UNDERSTANDING

THE EQUINE
FOOT

YOUR **GUIDE** TO HORSE HEALTH
CARE AND MANAGEMENT

ISBN 0-939049-96-1

Printed in the United States of America

First Edition: May 1998

1 2 3 4 5 6 7 8 9 10

UNDERSTANDING

THE EQUINE FOOT

YOUR **GUIDE** TO HORSE HEALTH
CARE AND MANAGEMENT

By Fran Jurga

The Blood-Horse, Inc. Lexington, KY

Contents

FOREWORD

Understanding the Equine Foot is a book that every horse owner should read from cover to cover to gain a better understanding of how the horse's hoof works. A marvel of natural engineering, the hoof has evolved as the interface between the horse and the ground. As the first link in the weight-bearing chain of the limb, the hoof is subject to high loading forces during thousands of strides each day as it performs its functions of dissipating concussion and supporting the horse's weight. These functions put the hoof at risk of a long list of problems, including laminitis, navicular disease, puncture wounds, quarter cracks, and white line disease. Our knowledge of these diseases and their treatments continues to evolve, and it is the responsibility of each one of us — owner, farrier and veterinarian — to keep abreast of the latest developments. Herein lies the value of this book.

The hoof is a dynamic structure that changes continuously in response to its environment. Climate, terrain, nutrition, and workload play a role in the shape and constitution of the hoof tissues. We take advantage of the hoof's malleability when we alter hoof balance or the type of shoeing in an effort to enhance performance, improve traction, or relieve stress in an injured area. Attempting to improve one aspect of hoof function, however, may create an imbalance elsewhere, which is a contributing factor in the high incidence of lameness.

Since the hoof is the most common site of lameness, almost every horse owner has first hand experience of a hoof problem of one type or another. *Understanding the Equine Foot* educates its readers about the structure, function, and care of the horse's hoof. Through understanding the inner workings of the hoof, the owner will be able to communicate better with the farrier and veterinarian, and to contribute to making an informed decision about the use of hoof manipulations to improve performance, or to prevent or treat an injury.

The author, Fran Jurga, is a journalist and publisher with a passion for the horse's hoof. She has devoted her professional life to seeking out new information on the hoof and farriery from all over the world. We are grateful to her for sharing her knowledge and enthusiasm for this important part of the horse's anatomy.

Hilary M. Clayton
McPhail Dressage Chair in Equine Sports Medicine
Large Animal Clinical Sciences
College of Veterinary Medicine
Michigan State University
East Lansing, Michigan

INTRODUCTION

Keeping the horse sound and at its athletic peak has challenged humans for centuries. Even now, with all that technology and new insights have to offer, equine foot care remains an inexact science. We still find the horse's foot to be akin to a square peg that we try to force into a round hole. Can the equine foot be analyzed mechanically, since it lacks true symmetry and the horse can make individualized adaptations to gait and stance? Can better foot care be managed biologically in order to help our horses move faster, jump higher, or round a barrel more efficiently?

For the past 20 years, I have devoted my professional life to learning all I can about the horse's foot. I have carefully observed and recorded the efforts of dedicated, caring professionals who work very hard to keep horses sound and to care for lame horses. I've sat up all night with anxious owners while horses underwent surgery, or were treated for laminitis. I've held hoses on pasterns, passed nails to farriers, soaked feet in buckets, and washed bloody barn floors. Every time I think I have seen the full spectrum of horse foot problems (and solutions) ranging from the best of care given to the soundest equine athlete to special care needed for a foundered pony, someone calls with the challenge, "You MUST see this one!" And they're right. There is always something to top the last one.

The more I observe, travel, and read about it, the more I am convinced that all the old curses, whispers, chants, and legends about horseshoes and horses' feet have survived for as long as they have for a good reason: the horse's foot is one of the last great mysteries of animal science.

Luckily for us, we live in a time when some of the mysteries are unraveling, thanks in large part to diagnostic techniques such as ultrasound imaging and scintigraphy. Sometimes it seems that horses are developing new foot problems, including the increase of "white line disease," laminitis, and navicular-type lameness.

As our biomechanical tools give us a clearer vision of how the horse's foot works, the arguments grow. How can we maximize the hoof's best qualities of strength and resiliency yet protect the foot's weak points? What are the best treatments for foot problems such as collapsed walls, sore heels, new diseases, and lamenesses?

I was pleased when I was asked to write this book, because it will be read by the people who need most to understand the horse's foot. It is the veterinarian's job to understand the medical and biological functions of the foot. It is the farrier's job to manage the foot mechanically. It is the owner's job to know when to ask for help. No one person has all the answers; no doubt all three have questions for the others. Only by working together can the three-member team help the horse.

If there is one thing that can be learned from this book, it is that the horse's foot is a unique, complex, and dynamic part of both the horse's physiology and locomotion systems. A lot can be done to a horse's foot — just look at any gaited horse or Standardbred. We need to learn the wisdom to understand when to let nature take its course and the imagination to envision what that horse's foot might look like if nature had managed the horse since birth.

An entire industry has been built on the horse's foot —

shoes, pads, nails, oils, sealers, medications, boots, wraps, frog supports, hospital plates, artificial walls, and all the rest. The mission of these products is to help us keep the horse sound.

The most important lessons for you to learn are which battles you should choose to fight for your horse (with the help of high-tech hoof care), and which ones your horse should be allowed to fight on its own, with the help of time off and "Doctor Green." The long-term welfare of your horse is always your goal, and there are tough decisions to make in order to achieve that goal.

Instead of working from the outside of the hoof, by building new walls, propping up collapsed heels, or injecting exhausted coffin joints, in the near future it might be possible to manage the hoof from the inside out. In the future, we will be engineering the hoof with surgical implants of collagen or cartilage, grafting coronary bands, transplanting frog tissue, decalcifying sidebones, and using arthroscopic tuneups in order to fix coffin and pastern joints.

If the concept of a bionic hoof is repulsive to you, consider the flip side: after a thousand years on the job, we have failed to manage the horse's feet in domesticity as successfully as nature manages in the wild. Our breeding programs have set a low value on hoof quality and high value on developing speed. We have created horses pre-programmed to break down, unable to stand on their own four legs without the professional management of veterinarians and farriers, shoes of steel, and boots of Velcro and Neoprene.

When owners stop accepting horses with defective feet and legs and demand better, more durable equine athletes, then breeders will be forced to create them. It could take generations, but the time is coming when horse owners will have experienced enough heartbreak, enough loss of performance, and most of all, will have had enough of watching horses in pain.

The countdown to long-term soundness begins the next time you pick up one of your horse's feet. Look at each one of them as if for the first time. The soundness of the feet affects the potential of your horse as an athlete, and is solely the result of your management. I plan to provide you with sound advice so you will begin an equine foot-care program to insure that you and your horse will go forward from today, soundly.

Fran Jurga
Gloucester, Massachusetts
November, 1997

CHAPTER 1

How Well Do You Know Your Horse's Feet?

The best way to begin to learn about horses' feet is to find out what you already know. You might know more than you think…or less.

On a plain piece of paper, draw a life-size image of your horse's right front foot (that's the foot on its right). Think about what shape the foot is, what shape the shoe is, how wide the shoe is, how far back the shoe goes, and how much of the foot the frog covers. Which way does the frog point? Where is the widest part of the foot? How many nails are in the shoe? Are the nails in the same places on the inside and outside of the shoe? What's the shoe made of?

Now, on the other side of the paper, draw the foot as it would look from the side. Is the coronary band level? Are the heel bulbs both at the same angle as the toe? Do the heels protrude behind the foot or sink beneath it? Is the pastern dainty or thick, upright or sloping? How much of the periople (the rough area at the top of the hoof where it meets the hairline) is visible on the hoof wall? Is the hoof cracked? Does the shoe have clips, a rolled toe, or built-up heels?

If you are like most people, you will be hard put to draw the parts of your horse's foot realistically, regardless of your artistic ability. You probably won't be able to answer the questions about the foot and its shoe.

If you ran into your farrier today at your local coffee shop, you might say, "You shoe my horse, you know, the bay with the little snip on her nose and one white stocking?" The farrier would look puzzled for a minute, thinking to himself, "There must be 50 bay horses in that barn!" Then a light goes on. He says, "Oh, yeah, the one with the little flare on the inside that we wedged up last time. I bet she's standing under herself a little better since then, huh?"

It is a farrier's job to know your horse's feet, not its face. If you learn to look carefully at its feet, you'll soon gain insight into your horse's athletic ability and learn to appreciate a good shoeing job. What do you see when you look at your horse's feet?

Chances are, the first thing you look for is a nice, round foot, and a sense of similarity between the four feet. You are aware if there is a discrepancy in hoof angle (i.e. club foot, flat foot, deformed foot) or if the horse is shod only in front and left barefoot behind.

You might have noticed that the front feet are more rounded than the hind feet, and that the hind feet might tend to point out to the sides, giving your horse's

AT A GLANCE

- Become familiar with your horse's feet.

- Know the special features of its shoes.

- Ask your farrier for a "guided" tour of your horse's feet.

- Keep photo records of your horse's feet.

- Keep records of your horse's foot care and of weather conditions.

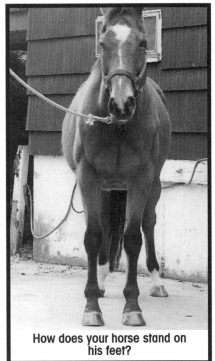

How does your horse stand on his feet?

hind legs a slightly splayed look, although the farrier has probably assured you that this is normal. You should notice if there are cracks in the hoof wall, if the angle of the trimmed foot is not the same as the angle of the pasterns, or if the frog protruded. Look at the feet like a farrier.

Can you answer these questions without picking up one of your horse's feet?

1) What size shoes does your horse wear?

2) What are the special features of your horse's shoes? For example, do they have side or toe clips, built-up heels, or toe pieces? Do the shoes have plates in the toes? Are there trailers on the hind shoes? Is the shoe creased? Is it a rim or polo shoe with different height on the inside and outside?

3) Do you know how many nails are in your horse's right front shoe? If it is an uneven number, are there more nails on the inside web or the outside?

4) What color is your farrier's truck? What's the name of your farrier's dog?

Time and again, horse owners can answer the questions in No. 4. They notice the truck, they remember the dog. They can describe the truck and the dog in colorful detail — much more detail than they can muster about all four of their horse's feet! They enjoy talking to their farriers about what's going on in the horse business, in the neighborhood, or in the next barn aisle. But they "tune out" while the farrier is working. After the farrier finishes, packs up all of the tools, and heads down the driveway, the average horse owner doesn't even know how many nails were driven into the horse's foot.

Most farriers like it that way. Owners' ignorance is bliss to them. They would rather talk to you about politics or how you did at an event than answer technical questions for which there might be no concrete answers. However, when something goes wrong, farriers are often incredulous that an owner hasn't noticed that a pad slipped, or that a clinch has sprung, or that the outside quarter was hot.

Farriers and veterinarians are professionals in whom you

place your trust. You might think it's OK to "tune out" and leave the technical work to them, but all too often you later find yourself scrambling for such information when it is too late. Ask your farrier for a guided tour.

Even though you might be an advanced rider or trainer, level with your farrier and ask for a little guided tour of your

horse's feet. Explain to your farrier that you are embarking on a project to gather information about your horse's feet, in the event that the horse needs to be bred or sold or leased, or in case of an injury or disease problem. Ask if he or she can recall any changes in shoe size, shape, or style in recent months. Most farriers keep records — that's how you are billed — and you

Are you familiar with the details of your horse's feet?

might find out that your horse was switched from toe clips to side clips, or that he went up a size in front shoes.

Many farriers carry a "hoof model" (be forewarned: it is the preserved limb of a dead horse) or anatomy books in their trucks, and will be happy to show you how your horse compares to a "normal" foot. Warn the farrier that you'd like to take notes for a little inventory of the horse's feet, for your own information, and that you plan to ask a lot of questions. Ask the farrier to show you features in each foot that makes it unique. Ask to be shown any warning signs of weakness or cheering signs of a strong, healthy hoof.

There are many factors that influence what your horse's

feet look like, including the following: genetics, training level, age, environment, medical history, level of farrier care, and your management style.

Your farrier will warn you that "There's no such thing as a perfect foot!" and might list off more detracting comments than you want to hear, but it is the farrier's job to be acutely aware of every feature of every foot. You probably have the same attention to detail in your own profession.

PHOTO RECORDS

The best time to photograph your horse's feet is immediately after they are trimmed, before they are shod. As the last step in their shoeing job, farriers often polish the finished

Take photographs of your horse's feet and keep them on file.

hoof walls and apply some type of sealant. Once shavings, straw, or dust hit the hooves, they will never look as good for the photos!

If your horse's feet do get dusty — dust clings to the sealant — wipe the feet with a damp rag just before the photo session.

Before the session, decide where the best place will be to take photographs. Do not take photographs in direct sunlight; light shade is best. Pick a spot under a tree or on the shady side of a barn. Make sure that there is a level, firm surface for the horse to stand on such as a roadway or concrete walkway. Or lay down plywood or trailer mats on the grass. Try to use a material that will show some contrast between the color of the horse's feet and the floor-ing. Dark feet do not show up well on dark trailer mats.

It's a good idea to label the photographs. Make six inverted V-shaped "tents" of white paper. Label them: "Left front," "right front," "left hind," "right hind." The other two should be marked "inside" and "outside." These refer to the inner and outer sides of the hoof, when photographed from the side.

Make sure someone assists you while you are taking pic-tures, or have someone else take the picture while you hold the horse. Always hold the horse firmly at the head, with the neck set at a natural angle. Do your best to square the horse up, so that its weight is equally distributed on all four feet. If you need to keep it calm, put a hay bag within easy reach of the horse, so it doesn't have to stretch or turn its neck.

The photography session should only take about 10 minutes. Take several photographs of each foot and experi-ment with different exposures to make sure that you get good results.

Your goal is to get four views of each foot: from the front (toe view), from the outside (outside wall and heel), from the inside (inside wall and heel), and looking at the sole and frog (ground surface view). Put the labels near the feet so that they will be included in the photographs for reference. This might sound unnecessary, but it can make a difference, particularly if the prints made it look like the horse has four identical lower legs!

Once the photos of the feet are done, stand back and take some general "posture" photographs of your horse at rest, with its head and neck in a natural position. Photograph the horse from the front so that the camera points roughly at the horse's chest (you might have to kneel down to achieve this view.) Photograph the horse from both sides, noticing where the legs are placed under the body. Have an assistant lift its tail when you photograph the horse from behind (aiming the camera just above the hocks). The last photo should be at-tempted only if your horse is trustworthy. Position yourself directly behind the tail, which should hang naturally. Stand on a box and photograph the horse down the midline of the back facing toward the neck.

Have the film developed immediately, and carefully attach permanent labels (marked with the horse's name and date taken) to the best shot of each view. There should be 16 "foot prints" — four angles of each foot plus four to six "whole horse" shots. Place the pictures in plastic pages and store them in a safe, dry place with other important records, such as vaccination records, registration papers, Coggins test, etc.

Imagine that your horse is injured at a horse show a hundred miles away. The show's veterinarian calls to describe the problem. While he is looking at your horse, you are trying hard to remember what the problem area looks like. You'll be very glad to have the set of photographs to refer to!

Plan to repeat a photographic session every six months, or more often if the horse is a foal or yearling, or if the horse is new to you. Dressage horses are particularly prone to changes in the shape of their front feet. As the horses advance in collection, they put less weight on the forehand; consequently their front feet might become rounder.

This photographic exercise sounds tedious, but there is no better way for you to learn about your horse's feet. Compare the photos with your horse's feet on the day the farrier is due to arrive. What differences do you see in the feet?

Many horses' feet change character between winter and summer. Some change in condition over the course of a rigorous show season. Sometimes, you will see "fever rings" on the hoof wall, often a sign of past illness or a dramatic change in nutrition. If you start training the horse in support wraps or boots, you might see changes in its feet or pasterns that will be visible when you compare photographs, but were not obvious to you on casual observation.

Photo records will also help if you are working with more than one horse. You will be able to compare changes that occurred in each horse and eliminate the problem of confusing the foot problems of one horse with another. You will be able to use the photos to discuss specific details with your farrier.

Save these photographs! If you ever move, or change farriers, or if the horse travels on a show circuit far from his regular farrier, these photographs will be your best evidence both to show to a new farrier, and to help recover what might have been destroyed by changes in shoeing in another farrier's hands.

Obviously, the photo records will be helpful to you if you decide to sell the horse or if the horse is stolen or lost. Many horses have been recovered because of identifying characteristics on horseshoes. Farriers who handmake horseshoes often stamp their logos or initials into the steel; most manufacturers will have an imprint and shoe size on machine-made shoes. Even nail heads, such as the distinctive "checkerboard" heads of American "Capewell" nails can be useful identifiers.

HOOFCARE RECORD-KEEPING

Secretarial duties might be the last thing you are thinking about doing when it comes to your horse, but you need to keep a record of when your horse is shod, and by whom, and whether new shoes were put on or the old ones were reset. If the horse wears pads, make notes when you stopped or started using full pads or rim pads, leather pads or plastic pads, and if wedges were used, what type and what angle. If the horse wears pads, make note of what the farrier used for packing under the pads. Sometimes the farrier recommends changing the time interval between shoeing appointments. For example, if winter is coming and you expect hoof growth to slow, you might want more time between appointments.

Do your record keeping in a notebook with a page for each horse (or on a large calendar if you have only one horse). Make notes of the products you use on your horse's feet and legs. Add notes when you poultice, and when you deworm. List the products by brand name. If you add or change feed supplements or medications for other problems the horse might have, be sure to write down dates, quantities, and any details that might be pertinent if a problem arises.

If you notice any problems with your horse's feet between shoeings, write them in the notebook, such as "thrush in right front seems completely gone" or "removed hospital plate permanently today" or "started training with grass studs today." When your farrier comes by to shoe the horse, check the notebook and see if there were any details you wanted to discuss, such as the size of studs relative to the shoe's width, or if there were any negative signs of stud use.

ENVIRONMENTAL RECORDS

In the same notebook or on the same calendar, develop a shorthand system for recording the weather. Very wet or dry periods can affect hooves, so you might not need to panic if you have a new horse and its feet seem mushy. Recording this kind of information will be helpful to you in the future. As the years go by, you will notice ways that individual horses react to certain weather conditions, particularly in the winter if they are confined to their stalls a good bit of the time. Some owners note the lengths of time of turnout and training, along with feed quantities and hay. Their calendars and notes cover each day and list hours spent turned out or in training. A serious conditioning program demands this meticulous type of record keeping.

Conditions in which you train a horse can play a role in foot problems or general condition of the hoof. Some horses can become accustomed to certain arena surfaces, particularly cushioned surfaces, and then will show signs of soreness when worked on hard or frozen ground. Many riders report problems with horses when they either are sent to or return from a trainer's facility. Working in sand or any drastic change in surfaces will require time for a horse to adjust. Keep notes of when you transport a horse to a clinic or training session, or if you take a long hack over frozen ground or a tarred road on a bright January day after the horse has only been worked indoors for the previous month. You might be surprised how helpful this information will be if the horse shows subsequent signs of bruising, stinging, or excess shoe wear.

YOUR HORSE'S HISTORY

Is your horse's health history shrouded in mystery, or is it written on his legs and feet? Scars, old tendon injuries, windpuffs, and ringbone or sidebone will tell you a lot about where your horse has been and how he was used before he came to you. Racehorses are particularly prone to a common set of leg injuries, as are former jumpers, polo ponies, or Western performance horses.

A horse bought directly from its previous owners shouldn't require hard work to find out the horse's previous lameness history, unless the owner is unwilling to share the information in the belief that it may devalue the horse. The owner has the right to privacy in this matter, but you might find owners who are willing to cooperate and who will turn over valuable radiographs or refer you to a veterinarian or farrier who worked on the horse during a problem period. Keep in mind that veterinary records and radiographs are used fraudulently by some unscrupulous owners and agents.

If you know your horse's pedigree, check other foals from the same mare or by the same sire, or even check horses from the same breeder. Problems often come in groups. While the jury is still out on the decisive rule of heredity in leg deformities and navicular disease, the old saying "Forewarned is forearmed" will help you avoid difficulty in the future. Making a trip to another state to check the soundness of a dam or sire may give you a picture of future problems you need to avoid.

THE MAGIC OF MOTION: WATCH YOUR HORSE'S FEET

Many lameness or conformation evaluations will include a simple walk/trot in a straight line on a hard surface, along with longeing the horse in a tight circle in both directions, also on a hard surface. You might hear a great deal of discussion about whether the horse "lands flat" (as opposed to toe-first or heel-first), "paddles" (feet don't swing forward in a straight line through the knee, fetlock, and foot), "overtracks" (brings a hind foot forward of the point where the front foot had been) and "displaces" (slang for prematurely planting a hind foot in a trot or canter).

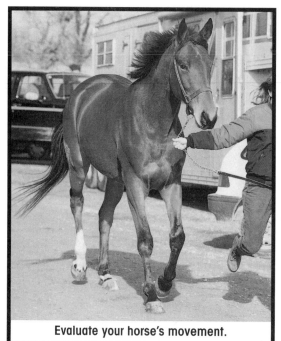

Evaluate your horse's movement.

Every horse has its own posture, its own gait and stance adaptations, and its own compensations for weakness, old injuries, pain, or the imbalance of a rider. Observations by others of how your horse moves might be helpful to your understanding, or just complicate the picture in your mind. The best time to evaluate a horse's gait characteristics is when the horse is sound, so that you have something for comparison in the event of future lameness or injury. A video camera can be helpful, as can simply comparing your horse to others of similar breed or sport type.

The basic tenets of doing your own movement evaluation are to have an experienced handler lead and longe the horse while you watch it. Make sure the horse moves in a straight line at a steady gait, with the head in a relaxed, normal position. Kneel on the ground and, if you need to, shade your view so that the upper body of the horse does not distract you. Video taken from the ground level with a zoom lens can be a real help, but the camera must be on a small tripod or sturdy box so that the lens is steady, and the horse must be led along a line of reference, perhaps between a series of cones.

A special aid to this visual or video exam is to wrap the legs in bright colored bandaging tape over the quilting so there is no bulk. Racetrack bandages work well and are thin. This might be a requirement if you have a dark colored horse, since the legs are difficult to distinguish and the hooves may blend in with the ground surface.

If you are interested in evaluating how a horse tracks or "displaces" at the trot, try wrapping the legs in four different colored bandages, and videotaping the horse from the ground again.

Working a horse in this way in a raked, sandy arena or on a sand beach, will give you hoofprints to evaluate. From your previous awareness exercises, you should be able to pick out the imprint of the hind foot from the front foot and decide if the horse is overtracking. Many large, immature horses will place the hind foot in front of and to the outside of the point where the front foot had landed. Overtracking changes in horses as they advance in training and collection.

Using a measuring tape, you can obtain a good measurement of your horse's stride, which might be useful in training so that comparisons can be made.

EVALUATIONS:
PROFESSIONAL AND PERSONAL RECOMMENDATIONS

One of the best results of reading this book would be for you to have developed an eye for your horse' feet that is objective and based on sound judgment. Most important of all, it will be your personal evaluation of the state of your horse's feet, based on the past condition you have seen, and a goal of what you want the horse to achieve athletically…and what condition the feet must be in to withstand the pressure of that level of training.

Many horse owners doggedly pursue veterinarians and farriers and ask them to voice on-the-spot opinions of a horse's feet or the type of shoeing. Please be aware that this type of questioning is a bit unfair to the professional, since he or she has no idea of how long the horse has been shod in a particular way, what the feet looked like a year or more ago, and what the horse's athletic career has been like.

Trainers and other riders and owners are quick to evaluate foot conformation and shoeing, and make recommendations, but you should accept their remarks with a polite smile, and a sincere "thank you." Only you have all the information needed to evaluate your horse.

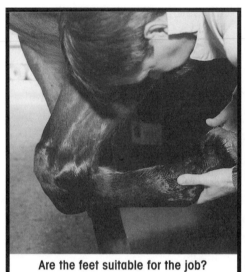

Are the feet suitable for the job?

It might be possible for you to hire a veterinarian or farrier to do a thorough soundness workup on your horse and provide you with an evaluation, but their ethical obligation is to remind you that their opinion is only valid for the horse on the day it was examined, and in the way it was shod. If you have a list of comments about your horse's feet passed along by a trainer, judge, veterinarian, or farrier from a previous owner, you should realize that time has passed, the horse could be shod completely differently, or the horse might have matured or advanced in training so that the information lacks validity.

Remember that what your horse ight lack in conformation or soundness may well be compensated for in heart, intelligence, behavior, or insensitivity to pain. What looks bad on a horse may not feel bad, and vice versa. Many horses with "pretty feet" have been to a highly-skilled farrier for creative management, so never allow your horse to be compared with another. Every horse is an individual, and deserves a fair evaluation with all factors taken into consideration.

PLANNING FOR SOUNDNESS

For some owners, the best course might be to say, "The future starts today." Instead of dwelling on what is wrong with your horse's feet, look for the strong points — thick soles or walls, nicely concave sole, or a healthy frog — and use that information as the foundation for improving other foot attributes.

Don't be discouraged if your horse has imperfect feet; many horses have made great improvements in their hoof quality when managed properly by their owners. Be aware that some of the limiting factors you have identified may be cast in stone, such as an angular limb deformity, and that you must not have overly high performance or soundness expectations of the less-than-perfect horse. Soundness is a blessing in a horse with a handicap to overcome.

CHAPTER 2

The Professional Hoofcare Management Team

In the course of a normal week, how many people put their hands on your horse or its tack? How many groom, lead, blanket, unblanket, bandage, or exercise your horse? Chances are good that most answers will fall into two groups. People in the first group would answer, "Just one, me!" In such cases, the horse is kept at home and the owner or rider is the primary caregiver for the horse.

A second group of people would answer, "Wait a minute, let me count…" Their horses are out for training or boarded at a barn where the owner or rider is not always present to give daily care.

Everyone who helps to take care of your horse has a direct or indirect effect on your horse's hooves. Think about the 13-year-old girl you trust to wrap your horse's hind legs at night. Does she apply the wraps at the proper pressure? Do the bandages ever slip? Does she always remember to pick your horse's feet out?

Think about those roofers working on the barn — the ones who let nails and tiny scraps of flashing fall to the ground below. How about the trainer's assistant who longes your horse each morning? Do you think he or she always remembers to put bell boots on your horse to protect those expensive egg bar shoes? And how about your friend, who generously offers to haul your horse to a show…in a trailer without mats?

If you are a natural-born worrier, you probably shouldn't own horses because they seem to be the most accident-prone of all animals. Chances are good, when they loaded Noah's Ark, one of the horses stumbled on the ramp and cut its pastern (or wouldn't load at all).

BOARDING BARN RECOMMENDATIONS

The best professional farrier and veterinarian cannot provide your horse with an appropriate level of care if they are always patching up problems that require first aid. It is your responsibility to make sure that, within reason, your horse is protected from unnecessary hazards and uneducated, careless handlers.

Unless your horse is in your direct care, a large amount of responsibility has to be transferred to others. If your horse is boarded out or kept by a trainer, you are still responsible for paying for medication and treatment whenever a mishap occurs.

Unfortunately, the quality of care given to a boarded horse is rarely equated to the cost per month or the deluxe appearance of a facility. Many horses receive great care at the smallest barns, where the tiniest changes in their attitude or the smallest limp will be noticed quickly. At huge boarding barns, you might find that the barn helpers see so many horses that they don't notice immediately when something looks different about one of their charges.

Before moving your horse to a boarding barn, introduce yourself to everyone who will be caring for your horse. Make sure that they know about any problems with your horse's feet or legs. Show them how you care for the horse, explain its current care regimen, such as medicating for thrush or flushing out an abscess track. If your horse is to be given feed supplements for hoof growth, make sure that the barn staff knows the quantity to be given and mark all containers clearly with your name, your horse's name, and your phone number. Mark the container "close tightly" or "do not expose to light," according to the manufacturer's directions. State clearly that your horse is not to be fed substitutes. Check containers often to make sure that the supplement is being fed and that the right size scoop is in the container.

Beware of barn help who recommend that you switch to products they sell. Also beware of staff members who recommend that you switch your horse to herbal products or racetrack remedies not familiar to you. They might be excellent products, but talk to others before you switch your horse over to the new product. Get the names of the people who are in charge of the boarding facility at different times of day (and different days of the week). Make sure that they are all aware of your horse's special needs and your "pet peeves" about care. Finally, mark all your equipment — from your hoof pick to your bell boots to medications and supplements — with your name, and keep a record of the equipment you have left in the barn to be used exclusively by your horse.

WHY DID YOU CHOOSE YOUR FARRIER?

A recent survey of horse owners asked why they employed their particular farriers instead of others. The answers were surprising. One group of respondents offered personal reasons unrelated to anything about the horses or about shoeing. "He's cute," was a popular answer, as was, "He tells great jokes." Other respondents employed farriers who were close friends or family members. Several people answered the same way: that their farrier had worked on their horses for a long time and they didn't want to switch.

Another group of respondents felt that they had little or no choice in selecting a farrier because they were limited by geography or by the fact that their horse was a special breed, or used for a specialized sport that required a certain kind of shoeing — one not widely available from other farriers. This group included owners of gaited horses and reining horses.

Another group of owners said they did not make the decision of who shod their horses. The decision was in the hands of their trainers or the managers of their boarding facility. Still another group said they had chosen their farriers because of their businesslike attitudes. The expertise of the farriers mattered less to them than the farriers' businesslike approach (whether they showed up on time or accepted credit card payments). A small group said they had

> ## AT A GLANCE
>
> • Know your farrier's qualifications.
>
> • Get references.
>
> • Find a farrier who fits your needs.
>
> • If your horse becomes lame, call your veterinarian first.
>
> • Consult with your veterinarian and farrier first before seeking a second opinion.

developed a good working relationship with farriers who gave the best possible care to their horses.

The survey turned up even more surprising results. First, almost all of the respondents thought that their farriers were "qualified" or even "the best around," but those surveyed could not list exactly what the farriers' qualifications were. Owners were fiercely loyal to their farriers, but often did not know much about the farriers' backgrounds.

Graduating from a horseshoeing school impressed a lot of owners, but very few seemed to know the difference between a diploma from a shoeing school and certification from a national testing body such as the American Farrier's Association. Very few owners knew what experience their farriers had in horse handling.

What should matter when choosing a farrier? When you choose a farrier, it is not unreasonable to ask for a resume — perhaps one delivered verbally instead of written — but a resume nonetheless. Here are 10 good questions to ask when you interview a prospective farrier.

1) Do you own a horse?

This might seem inconsequential, but it will tell you immediately whether or not the farrier cares about horses and if he or she will be able to empathize with your concern for your horse's well-being.

2) *How long have you been around horses?*

Believe it or not, some people graduate from farrier school without learning how to lead a horse. Some have never been around horses and wouldn't know how to tie one using a slip knot. However, they might be highly skilled mechanics or blacksmiths. At the racetrack, farriers are not usually required to handle horses much; grooms do that. If your horse is not stabled at the track, you'll probably expect your farrier to be able to get your horse out of a stall or pen. If your horse has any behavior quirks at all, this is an important question.

3) *How and when were you trained to be a farrier?*

Ask for the name(s) of horseshoeing schools and/or farriers with whom your prospective farrier claims to have worked

You should feel comfortable with your farrier's qualifications.

for as an apprentice. Many farriers claim to have "apprenticed" with different top farriers, when what they really mean is that they rode with that farrier for a few days, or they might have attended a seminar given by that farrier. An apprenticeship, or "working student" program, is the most effective way for a new farrier to be trained today. An ideal program would be to start as a "truck helper" for a few months (holding horses, sorting shoes, learning the routine); then attending farrier school (the most reputable programs average two to three months); then working as an assistant farrier, or apprentice, to a qualified senior farrier for a minimum of one year.

4) *What is your national certification level?*

At the time of this writing, there are three national organizations that certify farriers: the American Farrier's Association (AFA), The Guild of Professional Farriers (which is also called "The Guild"), and the Brotherhood of Working Farriers (which is called "The Brotherhood" or abbreviated with the initials BWFA). Each has different levels of certification; many farriers who reach the journeyman level are cross-certified in more than one organization. Most racetrack farriers belong to a union, or have some other testing process.

Since these programs are new, recently trained farriers are more likely to hold certification than older farriers. Many older farriers feel that their years of experience are a sufficient testimonial to prove their skill. Younger farriers need certification to show their skills and prove that they are serious about advancing in their profession. A quick phone call to any of the national associations will verify a farrier's credentials. Beware of any farrier who falsely claims to be certified or who bad-mouths the certification system.

5) What farrier organizations are you a member of?

This question has nothing to do with a farrier's ability because a farrier could be a professional student of hoof science and have no practical ability to get your horse shod. But if he or she does not belong to any organizations, a red flag should go up as to whether or not he or she is serious about keeping up with new products, tools, or ideas on shoeing.

6) What type of horses do you generally shoe?

Look for a farrier who shoes horses similar to your own. Farriers who shoe reining horses might not have the drill presses and taps needed to put stud holes in an eventer's shoes. A farrier unfamiliar with a particular breed of horse might not understand their special needs. For example, the need for weight or toe-length limits for Arabians or Morgans. Shoers of show horses are usually aware of the changing preferences of the judges in their area. For example, the preference of judges regarding the knee action of a show hunter.

7) *What experience do you have with lameness cases (or foal work, or other criteria important to you)? What veterinary practice(s) do you work with?*

As the farrier profession advances to the 21st Century, farriers will become more specialized. Your "primary" farrier might occasionally refer your horse to a specialist, one who is a lameness specialist, for example. Currently, there are some farriers who work as employees at veterinary hospitals, or who own layup facilities to care for injured or ailing horses, such as severe founder cases. If your horse is sound and in the middle of a busy show schedule, you might be happier with a farrier who shoes performance horses rather than one who specializes in working on lame horses.

If your horse has chronic lameness or a foot conformation problem, you might want to use a lameness farrier to keep up an individualized shoeing program. Most farriers will be honest about their lameness experience, particularly if "fine tuning" a performance horse is their favorite challenge. Many farriers will not work on foundered horses, due to the time it takes to learn that specialized type of shoeing. The failure rate for founder cases can be discouraging for a farrier.

8) *What is your billing/payment/record-keeping system?*
Many farriers expect payment at the time of service. You need to know this in advance, so you can present them with a check or credit card information. Other farriers send bills. If you require a receipt, make sure you ask for one, particularly if you are paying cash. If you want to keep track of what is being done to your horse, ask for a description on the bill — one that notes any special features such as clips, trailers, calks, pads, etc. Keep the bills for your long-term record keeping. If you have more than one horse, you might want to make sure the work on them is billed (or at least itemized) separately so you can keep track of expenses.

9) *How often are you in this area?*
Does this farrier make frequent trips to your area? If not, you might find yourself in a predicament when a shoe is lost

or the horse needs special care. Most farriers will insist on putting a horse on a schedule, usually from three to eight weeks, depending on the complexity of the shoeing it needs, the rate of hoof growth, or special lameness considerations, such as navicular disease. If you hear a shoe clanking and notice that it is loose, but it is still three weeks until your next regular visit from the farrier, you might feel frustrated if the farrier refuses to come back to reset it and tells you to call someone else to fix the shoe. It might be comforting for a farrier to tell you, "I'm in that part of the county every Tuesday and Thursday."

10) What options are available to communicate with you in case of an emergency or a missed appointment?

Farrier trucks once were identifiable on the highway by the smokestacks protruding from their roofs. Now antennas are a sure sign of a farrier's truck. Most farriers have cellular phones and/or pagers (both of which are useless if they aren't turned on). Trying to explain a lameness problem over the phone to a farrier's 10-year-old child is very frustrating, especially if you are standing at an outdoor pay phone at a horse show making an emergency call.

Make sure that the communication links between you and the farrier will be adequate for your needs. Ask for names of some of the farrier's customers and contact them for a reference. Ask them for both good and bad experiences they have had with the farrier. Ask about the farrier's business attitude. Many owners will explain that they use a farrier because he or she is either (1) so good with their horses, or (2) so skilled at keeping a horse sound despite the fact that "he never gets around to sending a bill until it's past $1,000," or (3) "she always loses the checks I leave for her and I end up having to write another one." If business acumen (or lack of it) is an issue with you, find a farrier who matches your needs.

Farriers like and appreciate professionally run barns, no matter how small. Most farriers are animal-lovers, or at least are so accustomed to working around them that they are "handy" with most animals. On another level, animals often sense a farrier's innate animal-friendliness, plus many are attracted by the smell of burning hoof or the taste of hoof trimmings.

Beware of farriers who show any evidence of behavior or demeanor that you would not tolerate in any other professional you hire. This includes threatened or actual rough treatment of horses, frequent verbal abuse of horses or assistants, bursts of temper, and any sign of disrespect toward you or your animals and property.

In the unfortunate event that your horse dies or is euthanized (for whatever reason), you will want to write a simple letter to your farrier thanking him or her for professional service, perhaps including a photograph of the horse, if it is appropriate.

In some cases, your farrier might ask for the feet of a horse after it dies. This might sound repulsive to you, but it is quite common for farriers to do this. A farrier will either dissect the foot or have it sent to a professional dissection preparation company like "Horse Sense Educational Models" for permanent preservation. In this way, the farrier can see what was on the inside of a foot that he or she had to work on from the outside. You have every right to refuse the farrier's request, if you feel uncomfortable about this practice. However, it is an important part of a farrier's self-education. A necropsy, or post-mortem examination, can often show the farrier more about the horse's lameness if there is evidence of damage inside the hoof capsule. This might not help your horse, but it might help the next several horses the farrier works on.

VETERINARIANS AND FARRIERS: WHO DOES WHAT?

In this age of caring for "the whole horse," both your farrier and your vet share the responsibility for your horse's well-being. Your vet is responsible for care from head to toe; your farrier needs to be aware of and knowledgeable about conditions in the entire animal, but will act only to the extent that it affects the foot. A farrier should not administer treatment to your horse in any area above the coronet. Even so, you will find that the farrier is knowledgeable about therapy for the legs and how to use boots, wraps, poultices, and liniments on the legs. Your farrier also can tell you how your horse's conformation is affecting its gait, soundness, or hoof capsule shape.

Farriers and veterinarians often work together to care for lame horses. If your horse goes lame, you should call the veterinarian first. The vet will ask you a series of questions, trying to pinpoint whether the problem is shoeing related or not. If the horse goes lame soon after shoeing, the veterinarian will probably suggest that you call the farrier to check for a "hot" nail or to reset the shoe with a pad under it.

With a potentially serious lameness, the veterinarian will take charge of the situation as he or she is the responsible party. The normal process has the following steps: The veterinarian provides a lameness examination with flexion tests, trotting out, nerve blocks, etc., as needed. If radiographs are called for, the veterinarian might pull the shoe before proceeding with the radiographs.

Alternately, the veterinarian will ask you to call your farrier to get the shoe or shoes pulled. You also might be asked to haul the horse over to the vet clinic for a radiography appointment, and to set an appointment with the farrier at the same time, so the farrier will be present, too.

After viewing the radiographs, examining the horse, and considering the horse's medical history, the veterinarian will provide a diagnosis (to identify the cause) and a prognosis (to predict recovery). He or she probably will confer with the farrier to see if the shoeing regimen has been changed recently, or will ask if the farrier thinks that special shoes might help the horse. You might have to have any pulled shoes reset by the farrier or the horse might need to go barefoot for a while.

The veterinarian will prescribe any medication and treatment (such as joint injection, special feed, physical therapy, etc.) and work up any shoeing treatment needed with the farrier. This might be done directly between the two professionals, either in person or by phone. You should not be the conduit of information between the veterinarian and farrier.

The farrier might have to make special shoes to help the horse, and might do special trimming or open an abscess location within the hoof wall. Technically, a farrier usually limits his or her work to the exterior of the hoof capsule. Most will not remove wall or sole without a veterinarian's written prescription. The farrier might ask that the veterinarian be present when the work is done.

If surgery is needed, the farrier and veterinarian often will work together so that special shoes can be applied while the horse is under anesthesia. The shoes are made and fitted in advance, then nailed on in a sterile environment. Such work is done during a ligament desmotomy to help correct foot deformities in foals. As part of the surgery, the farrier will nail on extension shoes or use glue to apply them. In this kind of surgery, as well as others, both professionals will provide you with follow-up care instructions.

The farrier might teach you how to remove and replace a hospital plate (the special shoe) or show you how to fit bell boots over glue-on shoes so you can turn out the patient in a ring or other grassy enclosure. You should be sure to ask the farrier what to do in the event that a special shoe falls off or gets twisted out of shape.

It is your responsibility to discern which professional to call when there is a problem during the recovery period. You might want to keep both apprised of how the horse is doing and periodically call to assure them that you are following their directions.

REFERRAL VETERINARIANS AND FARRIERS

It doesn't do much good to second-guess the veterinarian and farrier team you have chosen. There are times, however, when calling an expert is warranted. Imagine you're the owner of a foundered horse. You are frustrated because you don't think it is recovering fast enough. You read a magazine article about a new treatment for founder prescribed by a farrier in Idaho, and decide to deplete your credit card limit by flying in the expert to work on your horse.

To your surprise, your farrier is offended. Your veterinarian balks when you ask to have the horse's radiographs shipped to the "expert." What's the problem? If you have chosen the right farrier and veterinarian team, you should not need to call in any outside experts. If outside expertise is needed, your farrier and vet will approach you and suggest the name or names of experts they recommend for a consultation.

To bring in a consultant, you might be willing to spend more money in order to make your horse more comfortable. If so, approach your veterinarian and farrier to ask their opinion on who to call. Most farriers and veterinarians have been to national seminars like the Bluegrass Laminitis Symposium and are familiar with the techniques and talents of different laminitis (founder) consultants. The American Association of Equine Practitioners and the American Farrier's Association have worked together to compile a description of the suggested protocol between attending professionals (your regular veterinarian and farrier) and consulting professionals (specialized veterinarians and farriers brought in to work on special problems).

If you have brought in a referral farrier or veterinarian, keep in mind that your attending professionals are still the responsible parties for your horse. They have a lively interest in its well being. They should be kept informed of any changes in the horse's condition and changes in its medication and/or treatment. Put some extra work into keeping the lines of communication open by sending copies of letters and faxes to all parties.

ADJUNCTIVE THERAPY CARE

Most adjunctive therapy — laser work, massage, acupuncture, herbal or homeopathic medicine, or chiropractic work — does not involve the foot. However, occasionally one of these types of treatments could have an effect on factors contributing to lameness. Most aspects of adjunctive therapy are not scientifically "proven" but are widely used and appreciated by owners of lame horses.

If your horse has a foot problem, a therapist might not be your best investment, but you can look into how adjunctive therapies could stimulate circulation within the leg and foot. Acupuncture meridian charts show the flow of "chi" to the foot. Massage of the coronet and heel bulbs might be helpful in stimulating blood flow within the foot. Laser boots and

Ask your vet and farrier first about alternative therapies such as acupuncture.

magnetic boots and hoof pads are designed to send a healing or stimulating force to the foot either across the hoof wall or up from the sole.

Before starting adjunctive therapy on your horse, consult your attending veterinarian and farrier. In some states, a veterinarian's referral might be needed for certain treatments. Both your farrier and veterinarian will help you to decide, by discussing other cases where they have seen therapy work (or fail). They might be familiar with the work of different therapists, and might know of one who is well-suited to work on your horse's foot problem.

When a therapist is working on your horse, he or she should follow protocol, similar to the rules set down for veterinarians and farriers acting on a referral basis. The therapist should be briefed by the veterinarian as to the cause of lameness and should contact the farrier in order to understand any specialized shoeing that has been done. If a therapist is not willing or able to communicate with your veterinarian and your farrier, he or she might be the wrong person to work on your horse.

Use the same criteria for selecting a therapist as you would in selecting any other horse health professional. If your horse is restricted to stall rest or pen turnout due to a foot problem, consider working with a therapist to massage the horse's stiff muscles and keep its circulation stimulated, on the surface at least. Most horses enjoy being massaged. It gives them a welcome break from the monotony of confinement.

If you hire a massage therapist, ask for help and suggestions for stretching exercises you can do to keep your horse supple. A simple example is coaxing the horse to stretch its head back (flexing the neck) between its forelegs for a carrot or treat; ask him also to stretch to either side for additional treats. Another example is simply extending the foreleg while the horse is standing squarely.

Beware of therapists who promise to "fix" your horse's feet. Also make sure that the therapist has extensive experience with horses and is well-versed in horse anatomy and physiology. Sometimes human therapists offer their services to animal owners, but the results may not be what they — or you — expect. Remember, anyone who works on a horse without proper knowledge of horse behavior is in grave danger of being hurt. A lame horse can still kick!

CHAPTER 3

Team Work/Professional Care

It would be so easy if every horse came with an owner's manual to help the owner know its individual needs. Lacking a manual, owners must apply deductive reasoning to figure out what the horse needs to maintain — or achieve — optimum condition of its hooves.

Caring for the hooves is one of the oldest preoccupations that humans have had with horses. The Greeks wrote volumes on how to avoid lameness, how to choose horses with strong feet, and how to care for lame horses.

From the time of the Greek writer, Xenophon, to some current writers, all have introduced a good dose of folklore, misinformation, and a little bit of black magic into hoofcare textbooks. We are now beginning to learn how to care for the equine foot, applying biomechanical, scientific research. Even so, some soothsayers predict that it is too little, too late, since our breeding stock is composed of a large percentage of unsound horses.

This abundance of lame or unsound horses has recently created something called "the hoofcare industry," which had never existed before. A large chunk of the shelf space in every tack and feed store is given over to feed supplements, hoof oils and conditioners, hoof protection agents, and medications designed to fix what ails your horse's feet. Every year, horse owners spend more on hoofcare than they did the previous year. Farrier prices continue to go up. There are new products and supplements to buy. Hoofcare has even expanded into new areas including creating artificial, presumably beneficial, types of bedding for horses to stand in, and new artificial surfaces for arenas and tracks.

Routine hoofcare requires no special purchases beyond what you already have in your house and barn. If owners paid more attention to simple daily care of their horses' feet, it is quite possible that many "fix-it" remedies, fancy hoofcare products, and supplements would sit on shelves.

THE DAILY ROUTINE

As with most health-care processes, the most important aspect of hoofcare is to know what you are doing; to be organized about it; and to do it the same way, with the same tools, on a regular schedule. The care described in this section would be typical for a horse that is kept in a stall all night and turned out all day.

Taking care of your horse begins with taking care of yourself. Make sure that you are prepared to do the job. Check your feet before you go near the horse. If your horse stepped on you, what would happen? Sturdy athletic shoes, paddock boots, or at least thick, rubber

AT A GLANCE

- Clean your horse's feet in a safe, secure place.

- A hoof pick and a small, stiff brush are all you need for daily foot care.

- Notice any changes in the appearance of the feet, or any unusual smells.

- Keep feet and legs dry.

- Make sure you know how to use special equipment, such as studs and bell boots.

"Bean" boots should be worn. Never work around a horse in sandals or high heels, even if you are on your way to work!

If you wear glasses, make sure you have them on before you start, or that they are on a holder around your neck. Pull your hair back so it doesn't fall across your face while you are holding up a heavy horse leg. In winter, it helps to wear thin gloves under big mittens. You can whip off the mittens when you are ready to start, and your hands will stay warm for a little while with the thin gloves on.

Each hoof needs equal attention. Begin the daily routine with the hind feet, which are more difficult to lift and to care for. You then can move to the front feet as a reward!

If you have difficulty working on your horse's feet, plan a session with your farrier or with another experienced horseperson around to help you. Watch the "expert" lift and work on the horse's foot, then try to imitate what you have just seen. Ask the expert to watch you work on the horse, and to tell you what you are doing wrong. If your horse calmly lifts a foot for others, but won't for you, there must be a reason.

If you are intimidated by your horse, or if you feel that your horse is in pain and will not lift a foot, have a more experienced handler do your hoofcare chores for you.

Keep your safety and your horse's in mind at all times. Always work on level ground. Always use the same place if possible. The first few times you do the daily foot-care routine, have the horse held by someone who is paying attention to you and to the horse. Make sure there are no distractions. The holder should stand on the side of the horse where you are working. The horse should not be able to see its stablemates out in the field, because it will start to fidget.

If you put the horse in crossties, make sure that all the shanks, the clips, and the horse's halter are in good condition. Adjust the ties so that the horse cannot move backward or forward more than a step, but he still should be able to lower his head. The horse will naturally lower his head when you lift a hind leg. Make sure no one approaches leading another horse while you are working under yours. In a busy training facility or big boarding barn, moving into the wash rack area will take you and your horse out of the high traffic lane.

When cleaning the horse's feet, stay close to the horse's side. If you feel the need to jump clear if the horse blows up, do so, but jump fully clear of the horse's range of motion, particularly if the horse is cross-tied. Don't pick up the horse's foot until you are ready to work on it. One of the most dangerous things handlers can do is to hold up a hoof while reaching for a hoof pick or brush an arm's reach away.

Most horses are easily trained to lift a foot when asked. You might need to tug or pinch gently on the back of the fetlock for a second as you firmly but quietly command, "Lift!" Soon, the horse will lift the foot on voice command as soon as it feels your hand touching its fetlock.

Avoid rewarding the horse for lifting a foot in response to a hand on its lower leg, because you will confuse

Always have plenty of hoof picks.

the horse. There will be times when you won't want the horse to lift its foot, when you are applying wraps or boots for example.

Lifting the foot is not enough, though. The horse has to be willing to hold the foot aloft so you can work on it, and to support his weight on the other three legs, rather than leaning on you. Spend the time to reinforce and reward your horse for complying with the firm, clear "lift" command. Your farrier and veterinarian will thank you for it. If you ever need to medicate the foot, the process will be much easier because your horse will hold its foot up off the ground.

Make sure that you do not yank the horse's leg to the side; hold it close to the horse's body and work quickly. Your horse should stand quietly and not fidget or try to pull its foot away. Horses are creatures of habit, so always start with the same foot, and finish with the same foot.

Don't be discouraged if your horse seems to behave beautifully for the farrier and then refuses to lift a foot for you. Keep training the horse to respond to you. The horse probably is fully aware of what the farrier is doing, and "knows" that he is expected to lift each of its feet in turn. It might associate standing on three legs with the sound of the hammer and anvil, or the creak of a shoeing box rolling across the floor.

While they do their chores, some horse owners wear aprons or vests with plenty of pockets. They keep brushes and hoof picks in their pockets so they are close at hand. It's very easy to lose a hoof pick. Hoof picks should be bought by the dozen. Buy the one-piece kind, and paint a bright, unnatural color on the handles so you can find them when you loose them in the grass. The paint will also help you identify your hoof picks from others at a boarding barn (they are a much-borrowed item). Don't use a hoof pick as a tool to pry open everything in your barn; the point will dull and be less effective on the horse's foot.

The only tools you should need for your horse's daily foot care are a good strong hoof pick, a small but stiff brush, and a towel. If the horse has muddy feet, start the care routine by wiping off the mud with your towel. Then lift the foot, draw

Remove mud from the feet.

the hoof pick down either side of the frog from the toe toward the heel, and around the edge of the foot near the inner curve of the shoe. Always draw the hoof pick down and away from you as you work, that way if the horse jerks its foot, you will not stab its sensitive heel bulbs — or your own face — with the sharp point of the hoof pick.

When you use a hoof pick, it will loosen clods of dirt and bedding stuck in the horse's foot. You might notice flakes of sole coming off, too. They look somewhat like patches of sun-burned skin. This is the sole's normal shedding mechanism. The flakes should be very thin and paperlike. (Any sign of blood or a bulge in the sole is a danger alert that warrants calling the veterinarian immediately.)

As soon as you finish using the hoof pick, pull out the brush. Brush the bottom of the foot and check for bruises, loose nail clinches, or cuts. Many people have found nails embedded in horses' hooves this way, or found pus pockets that burst through the heel bulbs but were not visible under the hair.

Every horse's hoof surface is like a human face: no two are alike. Your farrier might leave the frog "natural" and fleshy, or might trim part of the frog away. The frog might pro-trude or be barely higher than the sole on a flat-

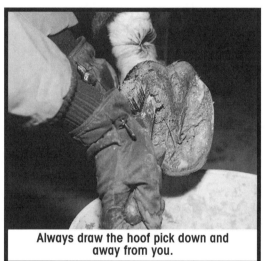

Always draw the hoof pick down and away from you.

footed horse. If the frog protrudes, make sure that the hook of the knife gets under the frog. Don't use too much pres-sure. Sniff for the smell and watch for the signs of thrush in the center of the frog or for signs of sensitivity and pain. Sometimes, small bits of frog, particularly at the back of the foot, will loosen and fall off naturally.

With the foot on the ground, brush the hoof wall in a circu-lar motion all the way up to the coronet. Pay special attention to the juncture between shoe and hoof wall, and notice the condition of the nail clinches.

Run both of your hands down the horse's leg from the knee or hock to the hoof. Make sure the horse doesn't flinch or show signs of heat or swelling. In the morning, you might notice small signs of a "bandage bow" if standing wraps were left on overnight in a stall and the bandage wasn't wrapped with equal pressure all the way around the lower leg.

If you practice this routine daily, you will grow accustomed to the normal diameter of your horse's lower legs, the cool feel of them, and the normal curves of the fetlock. Having established a norm, you then will be able to notice any heat or other danger signs. Do not turn out the horse if you suspect inflammation, swelling in the lower leg, or pain in the foot.

If your horse's hoof is not sanded for show use and the hair has not been trimmed around the coronet band, pull the hair back and brush the coronet in a circular motion so that the periople, or rough skin, below the coronet is visible. Feel the back of the pastern with your fingers, and make sure that you run the brush vertically between the heel bulbs, unless the horse is very sensitive there.

Occasionally, horseshoes will shift or twist, particularly if the horse steps on its heels. Sometimes when a horse paws, it catches a shoe in a dangerous wire stock fence. If it manages to pull itself free, you can be sure the shoe will be loosened from the hoof. If the shoe is falling off — for instance, if all the clinches on one side have been pulled — check for protruding nails and duct tape the shoe onto the horse until the farrier comes to reset the shoe. Put the horse in a stall and call your farrier immediately. Make sure that no nails can puncture your horse's sole.

When you are finished with the foot cleaning and inspection, take a few minutes to stand back and look at your horse's posture and attitude, and to let it relax. Don't forget a pat and a treat at the end of a successful work session!

If you are leading your horse out to pasture, always lead the horse along the same route, and pay attention to how it walks. This path should be regularly inspected and cleared of rocks, debris, nails, or paper that can fly up in the wind and spook a horse.

HOOF CARE IN THE SHOW BARN

If you own a show horse, you probably have little hands-on contact with your horse's feet. However, when your horse's show career is over, you might find yourself trying to keep a broodmare shod who has had her feet sanded for years!

The first thing that a show horse needs to know about hoofcare is that it had better stand perfectly still. Clippers and sanders are used directly on a horse's hoofs, and the danger of injury is great if a horse fidgets.

Clipping the coronet is the last step in a pastern clip. The clipper is aimed upward, against the direction of hair growth. On a light colored horse, the little hair that remains will expose tender pink skin beneath.

Sanding the hoof is a controversial technique. Many farriers feel it is detrimental to the condition of the hoof. Owners may choose to have the horse's hooves sanded only when photographs are necessary or when larger shows are at hand. Different grades of

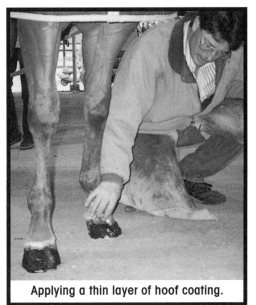

Applying a thin layer of hoof coating.

sandpaper, from coarse to fine, are rubbed across each hoof in succession. Once cleaned and sanded, the hoof is practically laminated with layers of hoof polish and finished with a product found in paint stores or art supply stores. It's called "clear gloss enamel."

Always apply hoof polish with the horse standing on cardboard or on a sheet of plywood. Apply the polish indoors, where doors opening and closing will not create a draft that can send dirt or dust flying on to wet polish.

When you apply polish, start at the exposed coronet, and apply the polish in a semicircular pattern on the anterior portion of the foot, stopping short of the heels. Do not polish the heels or the bulbs. Dab the applicator to rid it of excess polish, but know that any drips running down the hoof will be covered by subsequent sweeps lower down. Where the polish ends, be sure that a straight vertical line is created to make the foot look tidy. Keep the horse standing on the cardboard or plywood until all four feet are perfectly dry.

In some breeds, it is a fashion statement to apply hoof blacking, no matter what color the feet or lower legs are. To do this correctly, you must practice! Consider hiring an expert groom to do this for you, or else you might have uneven hairlines at the coronets, or get blacking all over the shoes.

Removing show black or hoof polish might require a paint thinner or other solvent, such as acetone. Make sure you know in advance what will be needed to remove polish. This is helpful information for you, too, when you find that you have it on your clothes and skin! Some commercial formulas have polish, shiner, and remover sold under the same company name.

Remove the polish immediately after showing the horse, and apply a hoof conditioner with lanolin. Do not let anyone use spray paint on your horse's feet to blacken them.

BELL BOOTS

Some horses tend to pull shoes often. In such cases, the farrier might recommend turning the horses out wearing bell boots. If your horse needs them, make sure that the bell boots fit to the farrier's specifications in order to protect the heels of the shoes. Many people buy and fit bell boots to protect the pasterns on the front legs from an over-reaching hind foot, and put the boot high on the pastern. This type of fit will not prevent the horse from stepping on the heels of the shoes. Fully fitted bell boots might not last as long, because the horse is likely to step on them, but the bell boots are less expensive than new shoes or calling the farrier out to re-nail a pulled shoe. Bell boots come in three types: the pull-on type, the "petal" type (with a buckle and strap), and the Velcro-closure type. Pull-on boots usually last longer, but must fit correctly.

Get bell boots that fit.

Know what a bell boot is, and what the difference is between a bell boot and an over-reach boot. A true bell boot looks like the end of a toilet plunger and is the same length all the way around its circumference. An over-reach boot covers the heel bulbs but is open in front, and the Velcro fasteners are up on the pastern. Many products currently marketed as bell boots are really fuller-circumferenced over-reach boots.

Run a flexible tape measure (the type used for sewing) around your horse's coronet to measure the size of boot needed. There is some guess work involved because the fit is variable. Most bell boots are approximately the same height, but it might be helpful to measure from the coronet to the ground to make sure that a boot will be long enough, as that is the area you want to protect. The formula is to find a boot that fits snugly on the pastern and covers the heel bulbs.

To pull on a bell boot, turn it inside out and pull the bubble rim over the foot. The boot will be upside down on the pastern. Just invert it and pull it into position. The boot should have a little play on the pastern and not be too tight.

Remember that a bell boot can "invert" or pop up while the horse is wearing it. If this happens often, you might consider the petal type. The "leaves" move with the horse and the boot can't flip up. However, the horse can rip a leaf right off the boot. For this reason, manufacturers include extra leaves. They also are adjustable, since the buckle can be fastened to different lengths. These kinds of bell boots are popular with owners of event horses and are frequently used in Great Britain.

If you buy the Velcro-closure boots, try to find ones that have two strips of Velcro, or those that fasten in the front with a long overlap. Some boots are sold as "no turn" models. High-tech models can have as many as four points of contact for the Velcro.

Bell boots can be an economical turnout aid for your horse at around $10 per pair. If you pay as much as $50 per pair for bell boots, you are probably buying boots that are designed for hoof protection during heavy training or competition, not for daily use in turnout.

Watch for signs of irritation from the boots riding up and down on the tender back of the pastern. Some boots are available with felt linings. The PVC or neoprene boots can create excess heat on the pastern, or cause a slight dermatitis to develop. Monitor the use of plastic bell boots carefully and discontinue their use if they are bothering your horse.

Clean the boots after each use. Rinse them under a faucet, then scrub them with a plastic scrubber pad, and turn them inside out to dry before putting them away. Do not use commercial detergents or dishwashing liquid on any bandages or boots. If your scrubber pad and rinsing in hot water can't clean your bell boots, try some Ivory liquid soap. Do not soak boots.

Bell boots come in small, medium, and large sizes, and manufacturers will generally equate the size with a horse's height. This is not very accurate; you might need to experiment a little between sizes and manufacturers. Once you find a company that makes a product that works on your horse, stick with it. Some companies now make extra-large bell boots for draft horses and warmbloods. Specialty catalogues often carry them.

Bell boots need to fit both the pastern and the heel bulbs. It is better to buy a larger size that fits the pastern correctly, and then use sharp industrial scissors to trim away parts of the heel area, or "hem," of the boots. Before you trim them, put the boots on the horse and use a thick magic marker to outline the area to be removed. Then take off the boots and trim them. Don't leave any jagged edges.

When cleaning bell boots, it is much more important to clean the inside, which rubs against the heel bulbs and coronet, than to worry about the outside. Always read a manufacturer's suggestions for care and cleaning. Some high-tech Velcro bell boots might be machine washable. Always use a mild detergent and dry them thoroughly before you put them back on the horse (do not put them in a dryer). Moisture problems seem to affect the feet of most horses.

"SOGGY FEET"

One of the most perplexing problems affecting many of the world's horses is that we humans do not really understand how the horse's hoof responds to moisture or alternating changes between wet and dry conditions. In the past ten years, many horses' hooves have gone mushy, and no one really knows why.

Some people blame the problem on the entire state of Florida, saying, "My horses' feet haven't been the same since the winter we spent in Florida." Others blame it on extreme weather conditions, lack of extreme weather conditions, poor nutrition, over-rich nutrition, feed additives, over-frequent washing and hosing, and heredity. But no one really knows.

We do know that many of our horses are being subjected to increasingly artificial environments, and often are shifted from wet pastures and wash rack stalls to super-dry bedding. The hoof seems to have a self-regulating moisture system that works from the inside out; either something is out of kilter in the mechanism, or the horse is getting mixed signals from the environment, and is releasing too much moisture through the hoof wall.

If your farrier comments that your horse has "soggy feet," ask him or her for help. Are there any new treatments for it? Does the farrier have any idea how to remedy the situation? Soggy feet are weak feet, and the hoof wall is easily deformed and could be more susceptible to invasion by problems like "white line disease." Nails won't hold as well in a soggy hoof wall, and shoe loss is increased.

Suggestions for curing soggy feet? Short of moving to Arizona, there isn't much you can do. Even in the arid Southwest, farriers complain about soggy feet on show horses who constantly are bathed.

If you do bathe your horse frequently, consider leaving the feet and legs untouched. Use a bucket of water to rinse the horse instead of generous hosing. Clean excess water off the horse with a racehorse scraper immediately. Dry the legs and feet with a clean, dry towel that has been washed in a mild detergent. Never put a horse in a stall with wet legs and feet.

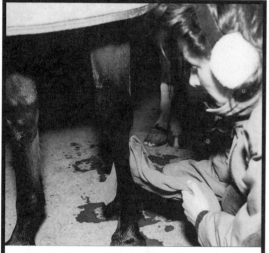
Dry the legs and feet with a clean towel.

What is your horse's pasture like? If it is wet and boggy, you won't have much luck hardening up its feet. However, if it is wet primarily along a fence line or near the gate where horses congregate, consider doing some landscape work to improve drainage. A simple load of washed stone might do the trick. A temporary measure is a few bags of mulch, wood chips, or even shavings. Do not lay sheets of plywood or plastic down over mud holes, as this is far too dangerous for horses.

Some horse owners insist of providing horses with a "mud

bath" spot around the water trough by letting the trough overflow, thinking that they are helping the horse. In reality, wood chips or an absorbent mulch would be more beneficial. Mud simply dries temporarily on the hoof and draws more moisture out, signaling the horse to send more moisture to the foot.

Alternating pastures is good farm management, but you might want to use as a criteria for pasture choice where the sun hits first in the morning. Wait until dew has burned off the grass before turning horses out, if they have been kept in dry stalls all night.

Do you sand your horse's hooves for showing? Sanding removes the horse's periople, or cuticle, below the coronet. Sanding is another example of the artificial conditions that we create for horses' hooves which could affect moisture balance.

How clean is your horse's stall? Sure, the bedding is changed regularly, but how often is the stall completely cleaned and limed, so that ammonia from urine is completely neutralized? If you simply put clean bedding over ammonia-soaked stall mats or wooden floor boards, your horse will still feel the effects of the ammonia, which could be drying out its feet and signaling the horse to supply more moisture to the hoof wall, perpetuating the cycle of over-moisturization.

Hoof-hardening agents were first popularized in Britain, where wet feet are a way of life. Unfortunately, such hardening agents contain formaldehyde or formalin, both of which are highly toxic and give off noxious fumes. These products are very expensive. Fortunately, they seem to have a positive effect on improving hoof quality.

The decision to try to clear up the problem by using products containing toxic agents is yours. Use caution if you are not the person who will be applying it to the horse. A spilled bottle around a child can be dangerous if the child gets the products on the skin or in the eyes. Do not put products containing formaldehyde in an unmarked spray bottle. Always read the labels to learn about the products' hazards before you buy them. Do not apply them to the coronary band or to any exposed live tissue.

Commercial products of this type include Keratex Hoof Hardener, Crossapol Horn Stabilizer, and "Sole Freeze." Some farriers make their own formaldehyde or formalin mixtures. Make sure that you know exactly what percent active agent was used. If you need to go to the hospital, you will be asked what was in the product.

Alternatives to the formaldehyde products include a concentrated paste made from Epsom salts and water ("magna paste"), Venice turpentine, icthammol, or iodine. Any of these substances can cause an adverse reaction in the horse or to the person applying it. Commercial tougheners and protecting agents include Tuff Stuff, which does not contain formaldehyde, can be used on the hoof wall to help protect nail holes and keep them dry. You or your horse could have an adverse reaction or heightened sensitivity to any of these products. If you apply them on a regular basis, watch for any adverse reaction in the horse's hooves.

USE OF CONDITIONERS AND OILS

The success of most oils and conditioners is based on the personal experience of the owner. If you find a product that is helpful to your horse and it is easy for you to use, you will be happy. What works for one horse might not work for its stablemate. Always make a record listing brand names and when you stop and start using a hoofcare product.

If you are using any external agent on your horse's hooves, make sure that none is applied the day your farrier or vet is due to work on your horse.

FEED SUPPLEMENTS AND "FLEX" SUPPLEMENTS

A large part of the horse-care manufacturing industry in America is dedicated to producing powdered or pelleted formulas designed to help improve hoof quality or rate of growth ("hoof supplements"). A second group is designed to improve joint mobility and supplement joint fluid ("flex supplements"). While both products might have therapeutic effects on lame horses and beneficial effects on sound horses, they are two entirely different types of products.

Hoof supplements are like concentrated vitamins for your horse. Different theories exist as to what a horse needs to grow a strong hoof. Different horses respond to different products,

There are many supplements for the feet.

possibly because of variations in deficiencies or palatability of the product, or quality of the raw ingredients. Owner error is often a factor in hoof supplement failure; especially if the horse receives the supplement on an irregular basis, or is overfed or underfed.

A tremendous variety of hoof supplements are available. They differ both in ingredients and price. Discuss your goals and ask for recommendations from your veterinarian and farrier. Some professionals prefer natural "herbal" products, while others recommend products they have worked with for years.

Do not expect to see the effects of hoof supplements overnight. Watch the area just below the coronet. You will see the first signs of new growth there, but it will take six months to a year for the new growth to reach the ground. Supplementation requires a long-term commitment in order to benefit the horse. Sometimes, a "fever ring" in the hoof wall will appear when supplements are started or stopped.

Flex supplements are relatively new to the horse scene.

Some include natural products like shark cartilage. Others have high-tech formulas of glucosamine and chondroitin sulfate. Again, there is a great range in prices, and little accountability for packaging, shelf life, or quality of ingredients.

Most flex and hoof supplement makers offer toll-free information numbers for owners to call. They will gladly send you educational material and answer your questions. Most manufacturers will refer you to a staff nutritionist or chemist, plus veterinarians, farriers, and owners in your area who are known to use their products. Follow up on their recommendations.

Flex supplements cannot repair degenerated joint surfaces, dissolve OCD lesions, or make a horse exceed its ability. No major studies have proven their effects, but many owners are convinced that they have a positive effect. Most scientists believe that these products work by supplementing the joint fluid, perhaps by changing its density or chemical makeup, which will help the horse "flex" the coffin, fetlock, or hock joints with less resistance than without the supplements.

The long-term effects of flex supplements are not known. Many owners feed the supplements as preventative medicine, believing that they are boosting the joint's flexibility and preventing future injury. No one seems to be willing to speculate about just how effective these products will prove to be for horses that have been fed supplements daily over a span of several years. Other variables include the mixing of supplements and the possibly negative effects of over-supplementation.

Variations in the success of all supplements include the quality of the horse's basic feed, pasture, and hay, the presence or absence of parasites (which could compromise nutrient absorption), the continuity of feeding, and the horse's individual digestive health.

Still another factor is whether the supplement is pelleted or in powder form. Many horses dislike powders, and simply blow out their nostrils into their feed pans, sending expensive supplements flying into the air. Manufacturers recommend diluting powdered formulas and adding them to grain.

When shopping for supplements, always check the "use before" expiration date. Don't buy products whose quality will be compromised before you are finished with that bucket. Always close containers tightly, and store them in a cool, dry place. Consider removing a week's worth of supplements at a time and storing them in a small plastic container. This will prevent you from opening and closing the main container more than necessary.

When you first bring a supplement home, check the scoop provided by the manufacturer and make sure you know the size of the scoop and if it matches the recommended daily dose of supplement for your horse. Do not take the manufacturer's word for it; test it against measuring cups you have at home. Make sure you know how many scoops you need for each feeding.

If you are unhappy with or suspicious about your newly purchased feed supplement for any reason, call the manufacturer before feeding it to your horse.

THE USE OF STUDS

Winter time riding and some forms of equine sport require extra traction. Riders often ask their farriers to prepare horse shoes for tungsten carbide studs. The removable studs are attached to the shoes whenever extra traction is needed.

Many jumpers, higher-level event horses, and driving horses wear shoes with holes drilled in their heels. Depending on the type of terrain and weather conditions, the rider will select different sizes and shapes of studs, or calks, to insert in the holes. The goal is to increase the horse's stability during takeoff and landing and to give the horse confidence galloping across snow, mud, or wet grass.

Studs are controversial equipment for horses, but the removable ones provide the best option for people who want to be kind to their horses' legs.

What to expect: Your farrier will drill and tap the shoes for you. He or she will position the holes in the place where optimum traction is needed and minimum damage can be done. Often, this means drilling the hole on the inner web of the shoe, to reduce danger of the horse stepping on himself and ripping the stud across tender flesh. Studs should not be used on any narrow-webbed shoes. Farriers need to be able to calculate the exact depth of the stud hole, the thickness of

An egg bar shoe with studs.

the shoe, and the type of studs to be used. Studs are a little more difficult to use in aluminum shoes because the shoe material is softer and could deform the holes more.

Some riders keep the stud holes packed with cotton or little plastic plugs made specially for the job. Others allow the holes to fill up with dirt. Either method requires a sharp-pointed "stud hole cleaner" to get the packing out before the studs are installed. Each hole needs to be cleaned, then sprayed with lubricating oil. Then the rider simply screws in each stud, tightens it with a wrench, and is ready to compete.

The rider must be careful not to screw the stud into the horse's foot. If the threads on the hole are damaged, this can happen with larger studs.

Riders need to understand that studs and boots go hand in hand. Once you screw in a stud, your next step should be to reach for boots that will protect the horse.

Many less-experienced riders equate using studs with being ready to compete at more advanced levels. The studs are a symbol, or a fad to them. Trainers should discourage this, and help less-experienced riders feel more confidence in their own ability to keep the horse balanced and moving forward, particularly with less-experienced horses. Young riders should assist advanced riders as grooms in order to learn how to use studs before attempting to insert and remove them by themselves.

Horses should be started in small studs and become accustomed to them before being fitted with larger studs.

Riders should go over their stud kits with their farriers. Make sure that you do not buy studs whose shanks are longer than the thickness of the shoe. Any shoe drilled and tapped for studs will also have side clips to help stabilize the shoe, since calks put so much torque on the shoe. The farrier will show you how to screw the stud in, and how to recognize what it will feel like when the threads are damaged.

Another problem with studs is that the rider may have removed all but one, and finds that one jammed in the hole, or bent. With an event horse scheduled for the show jumping phase after cross-country, this can create a dilemma. Be prepared with several sizes of wrenches, plenty of oil, and some elbow grease. Do not use adjustable wrenches to remove studs; use only box-style wrenches or a socket wrench. Many people keep all their stud supplies and wrenches in a fishing tackle box or small plastic tool box.

If your horse is wearing studs, be very careful about people crowding around it. Being kicked by a shod horse is bad enough; being kicked by a horse wearing a tungsten carbide stud could be even more catastrophic. Do not allow anyone to handle your horse's feet until the studs have been removed. Only allow people within your own group to remove your horse's studs, particularly on the hind shoes. Do not load a horse into a trailer with studs on; not only is it dangerous for the horse, but the studs will rip through trailer and ramp mats.

When the studs have been removed, carefully clean each stud and all the wrenches, taps, and hole cleaners. Oil everything right away so you won't open your kit one day and find out the hard way that rust really doesn't sleep.

CHAPTER 4

Hoofcare Emergencies

Nothing looks more helpless than a horse standing on three legs — unless it's a horse lying down. Finding your horse in distress because of a foot-related injury is an adrenaline-releasing experience, one that hopefully you will never have to confront. Since no one really can prevent a freak accident or medical emergency from happening, the best steps to take are to prepare yourself with first-aid information and medical supplies before such an event happens to your horse.

Foot-related emergencies fall into two categories: traumatic injuries and medical emergencies. There are many aspects of these emergencies that your veterinarian and farrier must take care of for you, but there is no doubt that the handling and treatment a horse receives in the first few hours after an injury can make a big difference in the horse's recovery. During those critical hours, while you are waiting for the veterinarian to arrive, you need to know how to help your horse.

PLANNING AHEAD

Let's take a walk around your barn and your yard. Where do you usually park your horse trailer? If an emergency happened to your horse in the winter, would you be able to load it? Or would your trailer be buried in a snowbank? Could the vet's truck make it to your barn? Do you have a gate that pro-vides the shortest possible route from your pasture to your barn? Does the gate have an easy-opening mechanism and does it swing easily while you are holding onto a horse? Do you keep a halter and a lead line in a handy spot? If you were in the barn coping with an emergency, could you hear the phone ring?

> ## AT A GLANCE
>
> • Be prepared for potential emergencies.
>
> • Have first aid supplies and basic farrier tools on hand.
>
> • Learn how to remove a shoe.
>
> • Learn how to apply a pressure bandage.

Training your horse to recognize voice commands is also a way to prepare for an emergency. A well-trained horse knows what to expect when it hears familiar commands. If your horse can be trained to obey you in normal times, and if you always reinforce his correct responses to your voice com-mands, you will have a much easier time keeping the horse's attention, and keeping it quiet, in the event of an emergency. A simple command like "stand" can be a lifesaver for the handler and the horse — especially when they are coping with a grim emergency; for example, when there is a one-gallon tin can sticking out of the horse's coronet. Training a horse such simple skills as standing quietly in crossties and being tolerant of people moving around in its stall are bless-ings at crisis time. You need to gather a few farm supplies and keep them on hand in case of an emergency.

As with most crises, the most important tools seem to be duct tape, a few old burlap bags, and baling twine. (Good luck finding real burlap and real twine. Both are becoming hard to find.) Some handy tools for hoof emergencies are tools found around any farm: a carpenter's claw hammer, electric clippers, and a turkey baster for flushing out wounds. I find that old pairs of clean panty hose come in handy, along with (don't laugh) a package of disposable diapers. When you

Some basic first aid supplies.

assemble the first-aid kit for horses, you should put in poultice powder, bandages, gauze pads, roll cotton, and vet wrap, along with scissors, tape, gauze rolls, and antiseptic ointment, etc. Keep another roll of duct tape there, just in case. Keep a cutting tool with each roll of duct tape; if you find a knife that cuts the duct tape easily for you, tape it right to the roll. I like to use a plain utility knife equipped with replaceable blades (the kind sold in any art supply store in the framing department).

COMMON HOOFCARE EMERGENCIES

Imagine yourself in the following situation: you've always meant to get around to learning how to pull a shoe, but there's never been time — and now your horse is dancing on three feet. The fourth foot has what looks like a pretzel nailed to one side of it. You're on a trail miles from home and the only tool you have with you is your wristwatch. Pinch yourself, and maybe you will wake up from this rider's nightmare. You did bring your cellular phone, didn't you? No matter where you are — on the trail or at home — two of the best tools you can have are a cellular phone (or long-range cordless phone, so you can call for assistance) and your vet's business card.

To turn the nightmare into a dream, a vet comes riding over the hill responding to your emergency call and immediately gives the horse an injection of anti-tetanus toxoid, pulls the shoe, and gives the horse other needed treatment. (In the nightmare, you also got scratched up and should get an anti-tetanus toxiod shot yourself.) Think of anti-tetanus toxoid as a stop-gap measure for extra protection, but do make sure the horse has an annual tetanus booster shot. If you work around the farm, you'll probably want to keep your tetanus innoculations up to date, too.

If you are savvy about caring for your horse's feet, it should not pull a shoe on a trail ride. Remember, you are checking all four feet twice a day. Included in that check is an examination of all the clinches and making sure that the shoe has not shifted. Still, a horse can and will pull a shoe off at the most inconvenient times in the remotest places. Usually, when the shoe is loose, you can hear it clicking when the horse walks. When a horse pulls a shoe by stepping on a front shoe with its hind foot, the shoe will rip right off. That is a blessing for you, since you won't have to pull the shoe, but it's not good for the horse, since chunks of hoof wall will very likely stay with that shoe! If you can, take a day-long course on emergency hoofcare.

Most of the day will be spent with you trying to get a shoe off the foot. Once you have learned what hard work pulling a shoe can be, you will appreciate your farrier more! Most barns will have a few rusty horseshoeing tools laying around somewhere; you might have seen them and wondered what farrier left them behind. Wrong! They are there because someone before you went out and bought a proper set of tools after he or she experienced the frustration of having no tools to use on a horse with a shoe

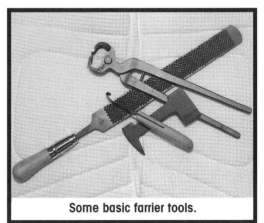

Some basic farrier tools.

half off. The tools aren't that expensive, when you consider how badly your horse can be hurt. The basic tools you need include a clinch cutter to undo the clinches, a pair of creased nail pullers to extract the nails, and a pair of pull-offs, which are used for exactly what their name suggests. Once the nails are loose, the pull-offs grab onto the shoe, you yank and twist in one motion. *Voila*, the shoe comes off! What a lovely dream. However, it's never that easy. Pulling a shoe is never an easy task, but the alternative to making it easier using these tools goes back to the nightmare scenario!

What if you have no tools? The most important thing is to have the horse secured in crossties so you can concentrate on the foot instead of concentrating on controlling the horse. Do not try to twist the shoe, thinking that you can break off the twisted part; horseshoes (good ones, anyway) don't break. Horseshoe manufacturers pride themselves on the un-breakability of their products. Sometimes at a farrier trade show, you will see shoes deliberately made into pretzels to

show the strength of the steel. A horseshoe is one piece of steel. In a nightmare, that strong shoe might have five or six nails sticking out of it, each one aimed in a different direction! If any one of them punctures the sole of the horse's foot, your problems will get much worse.

Any loose shoe should be removed immediately. This will prevent injury to the sole of the foot, in the event that the shoe comes part way off. If the horse can put his foot safely on the ground, let it do so. If you do not have any shoeing tools, find a tool that is something like a chisel — a putty knife used in painting might work if it is short and stout. Place the chisel

Most horseshoes are virtually impossible to break.

end under the clinch of each nail head and tap the tool in an upward direction with a blunt hammer. Remember that the farrier has wrung off each nail end and secured it by clinch-

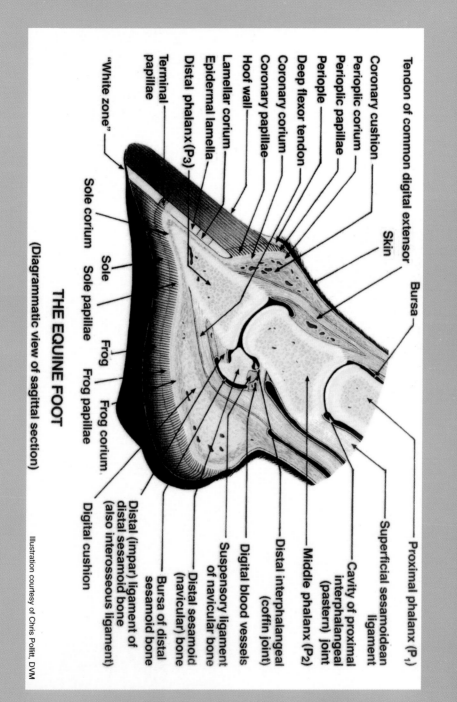

THE EQUINE FOOT

(Diagrammatic view of sagittal section)

Tendon of common digital extensor

Coronary cushion

Perioplic corium

Perioplic papillae

Periople

Deep flexor tendon

Coronary corium

Coronary papillae

Hoof wall

Lamellar corium

Epidermal lamella

Distal phalanx (P₃)

Terminal papillae

"White zone"

Sole corium

Sole

Sole papillae

Frog

Frog papillae

Skin

Bursa

Proximal phalanx (P₁)

Superficial sesamoidean ligament

Cavity of proximal interphalangeal (pastern) joint

Middle phalanx (P₂)

Distal interphalangeal (coffin joint)

Digital blood vessels

Suspensory ligament of navicular bone

Distal sesamoid (navicular) bone

Bursa of distal sesamoid bone

Distal (impar) ligament of distal sesamoid bone (also interosseous ligament)

Digital cushion

Frog corium

Illustration courtesy of Chris Pollitt, DVM

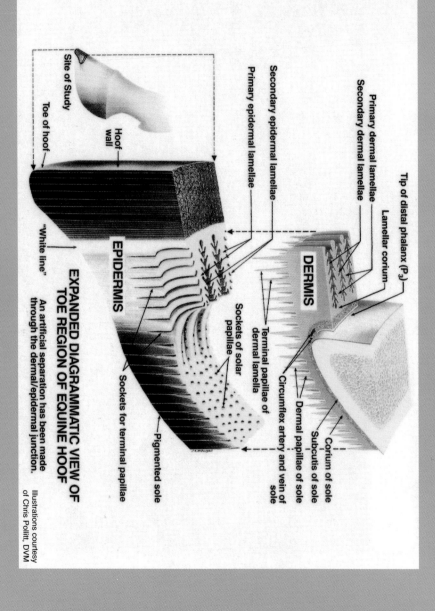

Tip of distal phalanx (P₃)

Lamellar corium

Primary dermal lamellae
Secondary dermal lamellae

Secondary epidermal lamellae
Primary epidermal lamellae

Site of Study

Toe of hoof

Hoof
wall

"White line"

EPIDERMIS

DERMIS

Corium of sole
Subcutis of sole
Dermal papillae of sole
Circumflex artery and vein of sole

Terminal papillae of
dermal lamella

Sockets of solar
papillae

Sockets for terminal papillae

Pigmented sole

EXPANDED DIAGRAMMATIC VIEW OF
TOE REGION OF EQUINE HOOF

An artificial separation has been made
through the dermal/epidermal junction.

Illustrations courtesy
of Chris Pollitt, DVM

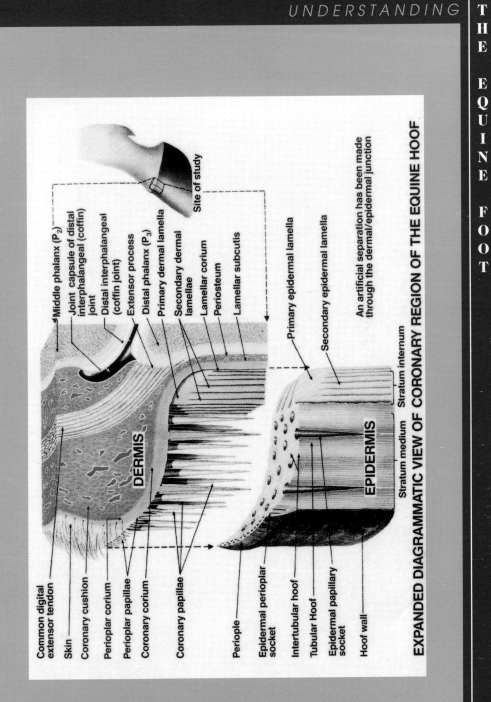

EXPANDED DIAGRAMMATIC VIEW OF CORONARY REGION OF THE EQUINE HOOF

Labels:
- Middle phalanx (P_2)
- Joint capsule of distal interphalangeal (coffin) joint
- Distal interphalangeal (coffin joint)
- Extensor process
- Distal phalanx (P_3)
- Primary dermal lamella
- Secondary dermal lamellae
- Lamellar corium
- Periosteum
- Lamellar subcutis
- Site of study
- Primary epidermal lamella
- Secondary epidermal lamella
- An artificial separation has been made through the dermal/epidermal junction
- Stratum internum
- Stratum medium
- DERMIS
- EPIDERMIS
- Common digital extensor tendon
- Skin
- Coronary cushion
- Perioplar corium
- Perioplar papillae
- Coronary corium
- Coronary papillae
- Periople
- Epidermal perioplar socket
- Intertubular hoof
- Tubular Hoof
- Epidermal papillary socket
- Hoof wall

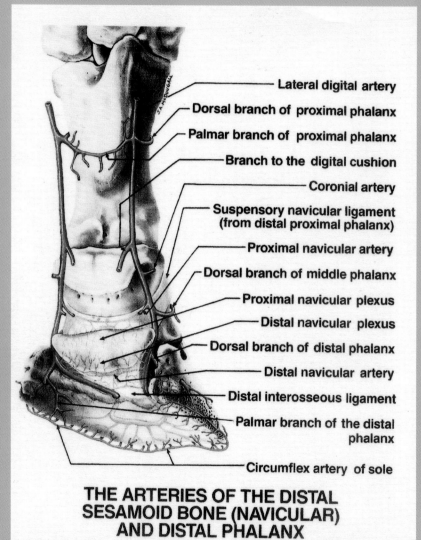

Lateral digital artery

Dorsal branch of proximal phalanx

Palmar branch of proximal phalanx

Branch to the digital cushion

Coronial artery

Suspensory navicular ligament (from distal proximal phalanx)

Proximal navicular artery

Dorsal branch of middle phalanx

Proximal navicular plexus

Distal navicular plexus

Dorsal branch of distal phalanx

Distal navicular artery

Distal interosseous ligament

Palmar branch of the distal phalanx

Circumflex artery of sole

THE ARTERIES OF THE DISTAL SESAMOID BONE (NAVICULAR) AND DISTAL PHALANX

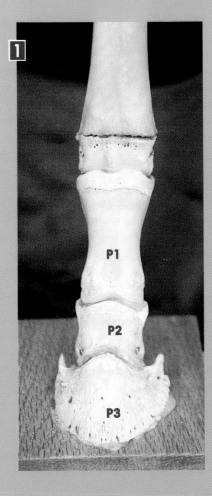

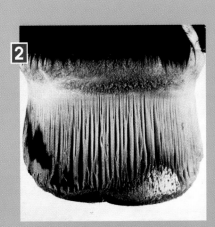

The foreleg of a young horse
(photo 1), showing how the
bones align; a hoof wall
removed (photo 2), to show
the coronary band and the
laminae; (photo 3) millions of
sensitive laminae attach
the hoof wall to
the inner foot.

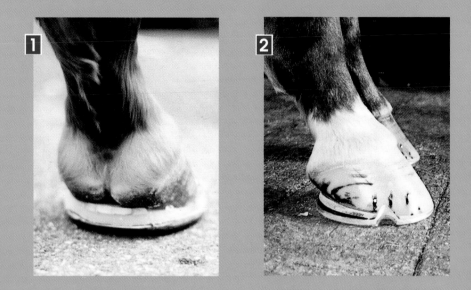

Egg bar shoes with wedge pads (photos 1-2); the shoe in photo 2 uses leather, which forms to the sole of the foot and is more forgiving; an example of a glue-on shoe (photo 3); a shoe with a pad (photo 4) in which the toe has been ground down to facilitate breakover.

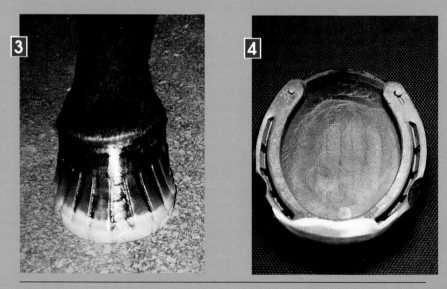

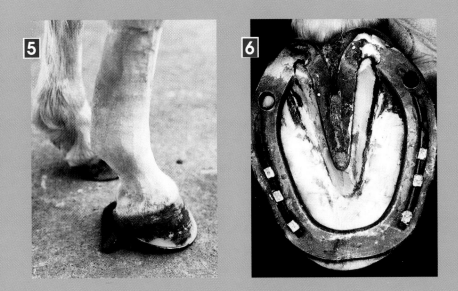

A patten bar shoe (photo 5); a heart bar shoe (photo 6), drilled and tapped
for studs; examples of modified heart bars (photos 7-8), designed to
prevent the horse from bearing weight on the sole and
worsening the original injury.

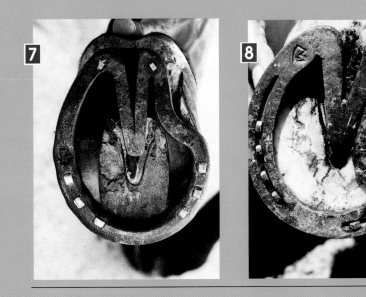

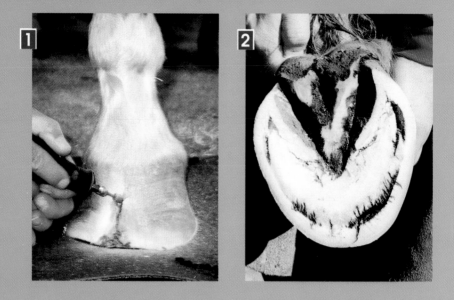

Chronic toe crack and hoof wall deformity (photo 1); seedy toe (photo 2), resulting from chronic laminitis; two different views of hoof wall disease (photos 3-4). The foot in photo 3 is from a dead horse and the affected areas have been enhanced. Notice the flat foot, atrophied frog, and diseased toe in photo 4.

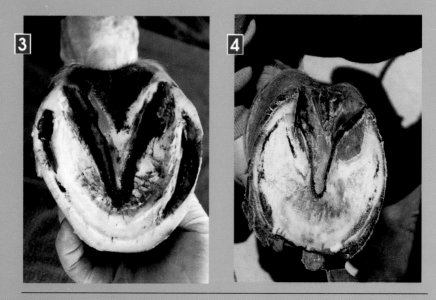

ing it (applying pressure to bend the remaining end up tight against the outside of the hoof).

Loose shoes often come unclinched easily. You might have a problem with one or more nails, but as long as the majority of them are loose, you can proceed with little difficulty. Once the nails are loosened, the shoe should be worked loose gently. Do not yank it. Some people put the claw of a carpenter's hammer under the shoe and pull...and they often get more than they bargain for, namely a big piece of the hoof wall! Start jimmying the shoe off from first one heel, then the other, and work your way around the foot, gradually, until you can pull the shoe right off. This could take a while. Be patient. Let the horse rest his foot, if it is safe to do so. Remember to take a breather yourself!

Once you have the shoe off, toss it out of your way. Look for any nails that remained behind, stuck in the foot. Brush off the foot and clean around the frog, looking for the signs of punctures. Clipped shoes can be a big problem if they come loose, because the horse can step on the clip and puncture the foot. Keep the horse in a stall until the veterinarian can deal with the puncture and the farrier can replace the shoe. If you think your horse needs protection, put an Easy Boot on the foot, or wrap it in vet wrap or duct tape with cotton or an old bandage packed under the sole. Remember to ask your farrier where you can buy a pair of pulloffs!

TRAUMATIC INJURIES TO THE HOOF

Horses do the darnedest things. Tough as their feet are designed to be, if there is a vulnerable spot, a horse will stick something through it. Some horses seem to have magnets in their feet that attract any sharp metal object that has ever been in a field. Still others are able to loosen a shoe (usually by relentless pawing) and get their feet stuck in fencing wire, through hay mangers, under stall doors. Sometimes, the shoe doesn't even have to be loose; the horse just hooks a heel on something and is trapped. Most horses, when a foot is caught, will panic, making matters worse. If you are running across a field and see a horse struggling to take down a length of fence that is hooked on his horseshoe and you can scream "Stand!" at the top of your lungs, and the horse does stop and wait for you...you have a wonderful horse.

Traumatic injuries to the foot can be bloody or bloodless. Don't be fooled into thinking that because there is no blood, the injury is less serious. Some relatively innocuous-looking puncture wounds create no blood loss, but the horse ends up being put down. Some horse owners are horrified at the amount of blood that a horse can lose through its feet. Remember that there are two arterial blood supplies to the foot. The entire hoof wall is lined with a complex network of capillaries supplying "the laminae," which, if spread out, would go on for miles. As a unit, the laminae attach the hoof wall to the solid bone inside the foot, and it takes a lot of blood to keep the area functioning properly. The blood inside the foot is under great pressure, so any injury to the foot can create a blowout of the pressurized blood supply. A simple equine first aid class will teach you how to apply a simple pressure bandage in the event of a major blood loss. It also will teach you how to check your horse's digital pulse (to monitor the pumping of blood in the pastern area) and what it feels like when the horse has a hot foot.

Injuries to the foot can be serious, no matter what part of the foot is affected. Let's say you head to the barn one day after work and see your horse limping toward the gate. It refuses to put its left hind foot down. As you watch, it gingerly flexes its hock, starts to lower the foot, then jerks it back up. As you get closer, you see that a big nail is stuck in the bottom of your horse's foot. What should you do? If your immediate reaction is "yank it out" first, then try to get your horse into the barn to flush out the wound, think again. The exact opposite is your best course of action. Leave the nail in there. Don't even touch it. You will be tempted to wiggle it or pull it part way out, but don't. The veterinarian will need to find out exactly how deep the puncture goes. Since a metal nail (or most other foreign objects) show up very well in radiographs, leaving it in place is the best way to insure a clear set of radiographs.

Call the veterinarian before you do anything else. Then, get help from whoever you can. Slowly help the horse to a barn or safe place where it can remain tied until the veterinarian has examined it. The horse might have been standing for a long time on three legs, so let it move slowly. Your veterinarian will probably ask you if the horse's digital pulse is accelerated (you probably know what it normally feels like) or if the foot feels hot. The veterinarian will ask you about the approximate location of the entry point of the wound. Usually, puncture wounds in the toe portion of the foot are less serious than those found in the heel portion, but an object can enter the foot at an angle at any spot on the sole and go right into the bones of the foot. The veterinarian will radiograph your horse's foot with the foreign object still in place, then remove the object. The radiograph will show how deep the object penetrated, and what sensitive structures might have been injured. The veterinarian will flush out the injury, pack the sole, and probably put on an Easy

Feeling for an elevated pulse.

Boot or wrap the foot in bandaging material. You will need to call your farrier, who will repack the foot, add a pad on over the whole sole, and nail on a shoe. Some wounds require what is called a hospital plate, which is a removable steel plate that is unbolted each time the wound is repacked or medicated. The veterinarian will probably start the horse on a course of penicillin and might leave more penicillin for you to give the horse.

An alternative to this scenario is that you are cleaning the feet at the end of the day and you notice a pus-filled hole in the sole of your horse's foot — an obvious sign that it stepped on something, somewhere, and that the foot is fighting the infection. In this case, you should secure the horse, call the vet, and check the horse's tetanus record. Your veterinarian might take radiographs. After the veterinarian evaluates the radiographs, he or she might insert a sterile probe in the wound to see what direction the injury took. You will be responsible for follow-up treatments, including administering antibiotics and doing poultices for several days.

The worst scenario is a puncture that penetrates the navicular area or coffin joint, or damage to the deep digital flexor tendon's sheath. Any of these injuries could be life-threatening to a horse. Surgery might be required to clean up the wound inside the foot (horsemen call it a "street nail procedure"). When you see your horse favoring one foot, examine it closely. A common site of puncture wounds that is often missed are the bulbs of the heels. This is a tender, exposed area. If the heel bulbs are enlarged and round, a sharp object — even something as simple as a thorn — can become lodged there or in the sulci of the frog and cause an irritation that will mimic a serious puncture wound. Never scrimp on having radiographs taken when your horse shows signs of a puncture wound. The horse could have stepped on something that has broken off inside its foot. Some horses have serious exterior wounds that are difficult to heal until a radiograph finally discloses a piece of glass or wood imbedded deep within the foot.

Puncture wounds are one of the most under-rated threats to a horse's long-term soundness. They often go unnoticed for days if the horses are not handled every day. Infection in the foot can spread quickly. Puncture wounds have to heal from the inside out. The original problem is often complicated by infection. Horses with puncture wounds require labor-intensive nursing, often for several weeks. Complicate the picture with the following facts: the horse might stand in manure all day, contaminating the wound over and over again, and the injured foot must bear the horse's weight as it flexes the coffin joint thousands of times each day.

LACERATIONS OF THE CORONET AND HEEL BULBS

Here's another horseman's nightmare: an old piece of barbed wire wraps itself around your horse's pastern or a piece of flashing falls off your barn roof and your horse steps on it, slashing its heel bulbs. Or your horse gets loose, runs down the road, and gets its foot caught in a culvert. Its hoof wall is flapping open. Here comes lots of blood. Laceration is one of the television medical words. People generally use it interchangeably with "cut." However, it makes a big difference to the veterinarian on the other end of the phone whether your horse has a laceration of the coronet or an abrasion.

The veterinarian might ask you if the accident resulted in a hoof wall avulsion. This last case is the worst case. A laceration is a cut that penetrates all the layers of skin. If you pulled back the flaps of the cut, you would see whitish-colored connective tissue. An abrasion is a less severe cut or scrape that does not expose underlying tissue. A hoof wall avulsion is a literal separation of the hoof wall from the foot. In a severe accident, a horse can have its hoof wall totally ripped off its foot. If only a portion of the hoof has been injured, the vet will surgically remove the loose section of wall, thereby deliberately creating an avulsion. Trailer accidents often result in hoof avulsion and laceration. If a floor board breaks in the trailer, the horse's foot might go straight down onto the roadway. If you are traveling at highway speed, expect to find a serious injury when you open the trailer to check on your horse.

With a laceration wound, your first goal is to apply pressure to the coronet or heel bulbs to stop the bleeding. You should know how to apply a pressure bandage on the lower leg. The severity of a laceration on the foot is compounded by the constant stress of weightbearing and movement; each time the horse shifts its weight, the edges of the wound move. Remember my strong advice not to remove a foreign object lodged in the bottom of the foot in a puncture wound? The opposite is true in the laceration and avulsion cases! The sensitive structures exposed need to be free of dirty foreign objects as soon as possible. However, the removal must ensure that no debris is left behind. If you are unsure how to remove the object causing the problem, leave it for the vet to remove. For some reason, wood seems to be the hardest material to get out of a wound. It leaves splinters behind; glass shards are also difficult to remove completely. Do not get out the electric clippers and try to trim hair off the pastern area to expose a cut on the coronet or heel bulbs. Leave this job for your veterinarian. If the horse has long feathers, as many pony breeds, Friesians, and draft horses do, tie the feathers up with that pair of panty hose you've been saving. Your veterinarian will advise you over the phone about how to proceed. You will be asked about your horse's tetanus status, and to look for signs of the horse being in shock. You should have an equine first aid manual on hand for these sorts of medical concerns. A good videotape on horse health also will show you what a horse in shock looks like.

Once you have stopped or slowed the bleeding and can look at the wound, you can flush the wound with a mixture of soap and water. (Use a mild soap like Ivory Liquid.) The easiest way to flush the wound is to use a clean turkey baster. Create a saline solution if you don't have some on hand (racetrack tack rooms usually have some around) in a clean, new bucket or a big kitchen pot. Just add a teaspoon of salt to a quart of warm water, and squirt this around the wound to flush the soapy water out of the wound. Do not apply any sort of medication to the wound. Your first reaction might be to pour a bottle of iodine in there; don't. Do rig up something to keep flies out of the wound. You can put the foot right into a clean burlap feed bag and tape it to the leg until the vet arrives. Don't put it into a plastic bag in the heat of summer.

Many are the horseowners who have fainted watching their veterinarians work the badly cut up feet of their horses. After the veterinarian goes to work and you know your horse is in safe hands, give yourself a break. Think of your own health and safety. To relieve the tension you've been under, go for a little walk breathing the fresh air, or head back to the house long enough to wash up and have a glass of fruit juice. Call your workplace and explain why you're late — and why you will need to take off the following day. Plan your trip to the feedstore to buy more first aid supplies. You'll need plenty!

You should understand that a laceration or avulsion injury might result in permanent disfigurement of the hoof. A common result is a raised bump, like an arched eyebrow, in the coronet. Sometimes, a hoof will be unable to retain its normal shape, particularly if casting material is applied. The new hoof wall might seem straighter than the old wall, making the foot asymmetric. This will be a long-term project for your farrier to work on. Using hoof repair compounds, the farrier should be able to disguise the injury cosmetically if it is detrimental to your use of the horse. Many people do not truly appreciate the horse's foot until they see a horse recover from a serious laceration or avulsion.

Often an avulsion rips off the wall and takes the coronet with it. Under the coronet is the coronary band, the main blood supply to the hoof wall. While it might not be as pretty as the original hoof, the foot will grow a new coronary band and a new hoof. These remarkable structures regenerate completely. If you watch this process over a few months, you will be amazed. Another thing that will amaze you is the range of therapeutic products available to help your horse recover, including glue-on shoes for hoof avulsion cases, special hospital plates, and antiseptic hoof packings (a popular brand is called "Sole Pack") that go against the sole and frog and help prevent infection and deterioration of the sole.

I have watched a farrier rig an ingenious drainage tube made with narrow, plastic aquarium tubing that was laced inside an artificial hoof wall, which made flushing out the wound an easy procedure. Go to any major equine surgery unit or to a veterinary teaching hospital and you will see horses with very creative "rigs" to allow for drainage, medication, or protection.

With most major trauma cases involving a horse's foot, healing will require bandaging, special shoes, pads, and lots of nursing. However, you need to be aware that the horse might obviously or subtly adjust weightbearing to avoid overstressing the injured foot. The injured horse might put more weight on the bilateral leg. This often can lead to a mechanical laminitis situation in the "good" leg, a common complication of horses recovering from leg fractures. Be sure to ask your vet and farrier if you need to worry about laminitis in the opposite foot.

EMERGENCY PREPARATIONS

A note about disasters: If you and your horse have ever survived a major natural disaster, such as a hurricane, flood, tornado, or fire, you know the importance of having a barn well-stocked with first aid supplies. You must become well-armed with knowledge in order to cope with a natural disaster. The field of equine rescue is a new, but important one. I recommend that you add to your required reading list a little book called *What Do I Do with My Horse in Fire, Flood, and/or Earthquake?* by Stephanie Abronson and Joe Goodman. It is available for $2.50 from Stephanie Abronson, 543 Cold Canyon Road, Monte Nido, CA 91302. This little book is based on the first-hand experiences of horse owners who helped horses during recent earthquakes and fires in

California. The book contains information about setting up your barn, pasture, first aid kit, and contains emergency plans. Reading through it and following the authors' suggestions might be the most important thing you ever do for your animals.

Equine Rescue Techniques: Instruction for Emergency Response Professionals by Kanee Haertel and Craig Tisdale, published as a public service by Purina Mills, is another excellent publication with advice on emergencies. It was designed as a handbook for municipal fire-and-rescue personnel to learn how to extricate horses from dangerous situations, including trailer accidents. A copy of this little publication should be in the glove box of your truck any time you haul your horses with a trailer. Although you may find reading about possible disasters on the road is enough to make you want to stay home!

MEDICAL EMERGENCIES AFFECTING THE FOOT

Laminitis

Any one of the diseases grouped under the heading of laminitis is the equivalent of a full-fledged disaster for most horses. The subject is an extremely complex medical issue that has little to do with the foot itself, other than that the foot bears the brunt of the disease. Laminitis can be a disease, or a secondary episode of another

A pony suffering from laminitis.

medical problem, such as Potomac horse fever, foaling problems, pituitary tumors ("Cushing's Syndrome"), or almost any toxic condition in the horse's system that causes an allergic reaction, such as the ingestion of poisonous plants like the black walnut.

The ways that the disease affects the feet are just as varied

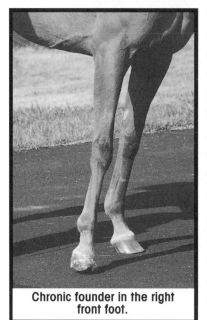

Chronic founder in the right front foot.

as the causes of laminitis. When they are affected by laminitis, some horses show no signs of lameness, while others are unable to walk. Some horses never recover from the initial onset of lameness. Others seem to suffer recurring bouts and go lame, then recover with amazing resiliency. If anyone tells you that they know all about laminitis, or how to fix a laminitic horse, smile politely and change the subject, quickly. It would be easy to write a book just on laminitis and how it affects horses' feet. What follows is a simplified view of laminitis. If you have a horse that suffers from laminitis, you will need first-rate, in-depth reference materials on laminitis plus advice from your veterinarian relevant to your horse's individual case and prognosis.

What is laminitis?

Laminitis is a major insult to the horse's system; it can be caused by a long list of problems. The most common cause is grain (carbohydrate) overload. The next day, the horse is in so much pain that it can't walk. That's classic laminitis. Most of the cases veterinarians see now are not the classic ones. They are the disastrous ones. An example of disastrous laminitis would be a horse having a toxic reaction to a medication, usually from some type of steroid.

By whatever mechanism in the horse's blood, endocrine, or nervous system (or combination of systems) causes the problem, the feet bear the brunt of the toxic insult. The hoof wall is attached to the coffin bone (P3) by a network of fibers called "laminae." Think of your hands, wearing gloves. The glove on your right hand is red, full of blood, and covers the coffin bone. The glove on your left hand is black, insensitive, and covers the inside of the hoof wall. Join your hands by interweaving your fingers; this is the bone-to-hoof wall bond. Imagine hundreds of smaller fingers coming out of each of your main fingers; these would be "secondary laminae" that create an even stronger bond. Each lamina is surrounded by an envelope called a "basement membrane." For some reason, when laminitis strikes, the basement membrane in the foot is destroyed. In some cases, it is only partially destroyed and the tissues quickly regenerate. In other cases, the laminae might be destroyed only in the toe area. If enough laminae let go, the coffin bone, which is part of the weightbearing system of the leg, becomes unstable.

> ## AT A GLANCE
>
> • Laminitis is an inflammation of the sensitive tissue inside the foot.
>
> • Symptoms can include a bounding pulse, reluctance to move, and standing with both front feet far forward and hind feet under the belly.
>
> • Laminitis often is secondary to other problems, such as a reaction to steroids or Potomac horse fever.
>
> • If you suspect your horse is suffering from laminitis, call your veterinarian immediately.

To oversimplify once more, the deep digital flexor tendon runs down the back of the pastern and attaches to the bottom of the coffin bone. It pulls the bone upwards and backwards in the hoof capsule, but is usually offset by the stabilizing force of the extensor tendon at the crown of the coffin bone and the laminae network all around the circumference of the coffin bone. When the laminae let go, the bone responds to the pull of the tendon and is pulled away from the hoof wall.

To evaluate the amount of damage done by the laminitis insult, veterinarians take lateral (side view) radiographs and check the angulation of the coffin bone inside the foot. Normally, the coffin bone and the hoof wall are parallel. If the dorsal (front) edge of the bone seems tipped downward, out of alignment with the toe of the hoof wall, they say it has "rotated" out of its proper position. In some laminitis cases, all of the basement membranes are destroyed more or less at once, and the hoof capsule lets go of the bones. The boney column literally "sinks" under the horse's weight (hence the term "a sinker case"). In such a case, the horse's hoof walls might just let go, which is called "sloughing the hoof."

Another grim problem with laminitis cases is that the horses often develop laminitis without showing outward signs of distress at first. It could be as much as 24 hours before the horse shows signs of discomfort. By then, a lot of the damage is irreversable. All the medical and mechanical treatments can do is to prevent further damage. For too many horses, such treatments are too little, too late.

Signs of laminitis

A laminitic horse shows classic signs, usually in both front feet. However, only one foot might be affected — or all four. First, there will be a bounding pulse; you sometimes can see the pulse at the pastern without even feeling for it. If you place your hand on the hoof wall, you can feel how warm it is. The horse will resist your commands to be lead.

By "pointing," the horse might exhibit the classic stance of a foundered horse. It will extend the hind feet as far forward as possible under the body and simultaneously extend its front feet, so that it rests most of its weight on the hind end. The horse will pivot on its hind feet and shuffle along stiffly, placing its weight on the heels of its front feet. Watching a foundered horse painfully move along can be a very unsettling and distressing experience for the uninitiated.

If the horse has had an extreme reaction, and "sinking" has taken place, the coronet will seem to have dropped inside the foot. If you place your hand at the top of the hoof capsule, you can feel a shelf where the coronary band used to be. If you see your horse exhibit any of these signs, call your veterinarian immediately.

Treatment of laminitis

Many treatments for laminitis are used, all depending on the case, the circumstances, and the preferences of the medical professionals involved. You can expect your horse to receive non-steroidal, anti-inflammatory medication immediately, and for the shoes to be pulled and radiographs taken. This is the time when your old radiographs should be dusted off and brought out for comparison to see how much, if any, damage has been done.

The immediate mechanical treatment of laminitis might seem simple. A frog support device made from blocks of thick styrofoam can be taped onto the foot using duct tape or vet-wrap. The veterinarian might advise you to prepare a hospital stall with a sand floor, or to add a few more bales of shavings to an existing stall. He or she will also ask you to put the horse on a "lite" diet, probably consisting just of timothy or "grass" hay, to avoid any further insult from the carbohydrates in

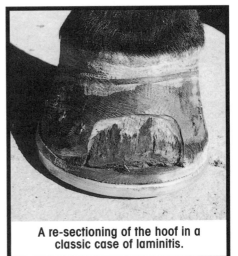

A re-sectioning of the hoof in a classic case of laminitis.

feed, alfalfa, or oats. The mechanical treatment of laminitis is also a personal preference, and usually will be decided by the veterinarian and farrier.

You will need to consult with your farrier about how he or she feels about working on a foundered horse. Many farriers are not willing to spend the time finetuning the hoofcare to keep the horse comfortable, and would rather turn the horse over to a laminitis specialist who will be able to spend the time with your horse. This is becoming increasingly common around the United States. If you are lucky, there will be such a farrier in your area. If not, you might want to board your horse at a vet clinic with a staff farrier (another increasingly common arrangement) where the horse will be checked daily by the farrier.

What is founder?

Laminitis is the technical name for the disease. Acute laminitis marks the onset of the disease. This is the early stage of the disease, when the damage is done. "Founder" is a commonly overused word encompassing all aspects of laminitis. Technically, it means the state of instability, when the coffin bone is vulnerable. A horse that has had a serious bout of laminitis might be susceptible to the disease again days, weeks, or years later. Horses with recurrent laminitis are generally said to have "chronic founder." The recurrences can be mild or severe. Ponies are especially susceptible to chronic founder episodes.

What to expect

Always expect the worst when a horse has been hit hard by laminitis, at least until our dedicated researchers learn more about how to treat it successfully. Remember that it was chronic founder that ended the life of the great race-horse and stallion, Secretariat, along with thousands of other performance horses and backyard "pasture pets." You should not let veterinarians and farriers give you false hope for miracle cures. All you can do is get the best treatment available for your horse, make sure it is on an excellent quality feed supplement to stimulate healthy new hoof growth, and wait and see how the horse recovers.

Recovery with a foundered horse means that the foot is stabilized so that a new hoof can grow down. Different techniques are sometimes used to remove part of the hoof wall, or to relieve pressure on the wall. Special shoes, particularly heart-bar shoes, are sometimes successful in redirecting stress from the toe of the hoof wall, but the shoes must be applied by an expert farrier. While many horses do fine without them, many are the horses of whom are said, "We probably should have tried a heart-bar..."

Aside from "sinkers," the worst cases of laminitis are the ones where the coffin bone rotates and the foot becomes riddled with abscesses. The sole prolapses (drops). In such cases, it is hard to know which problem to treat first. It is equally hard to know when to give up; many vets and farriers euphemistically say, "The horse told me to give up."

Horses seem to have varying thresholds of pain and wills to live. Always do what you think is best for the horse, and for your conscience. The miracle cases that you hear about — horses winning at shows after recovering from laminitis — are by far the exception to the rule. Hopefully, it won't always be that way.

CHAPTER 5

Problems of the Equine Foot/Glossary

The goal of this book has been to help you appreciate the unique characteristics of your horse's feet as you provide routine but important care that will help prevent lameness and injury. Now that you have developed stable management skills and you have found a crack team of professionals to work with you to care for your horse's feet, you need to appreciate how fragile and fantastic the horse's foot is. It is the structure responsible for keeping the horse in motion, but it is also a portion of its anatomy that must function properly, or it stops the horse dead in its tracks. Don't let that happen to your horse!

Each of the sections in this chapter covers an important component of the equine foot and/or a specific foot problem that can beset the horse. Each section includes a description and tips on how to recognize the problem, some idea of the treatment your veterinarian and farrier must do, and the prognosis. They follow in alphabetical order.

ABSCESS

An abscess, or pus pocket, is a reaction to a bacterial irritation in the foot. The body's endocrine system sends white blood cells to the point of irritation. They act like commandos, defending the body against foreign agents. Pus and gas are by-products of the battle. When they are trapped between the hoof wall and the coffin bone, there is literally nowhere for the pus and gas to go except to follow a path of least resistance out of the foot to daylight. In some cases, this means the pus and gas pockets migrate up the hoof wall and break out at the coronary band (this is commonly called a "gravel"). In other cases, the pus and gas erupt at the bulbs of the heels. If the pus pocket is under the sole, it is called a subsolar abscess. The vet or farrier will open a drainage tract by carving through the sole.

Abscesses are one of the most common side-effects of severe laminitis. Multiple and simultaneous abscesses are common in such cases.

Warning signs: These include heat in the coronary band, hoof wall, or sole and/or sudden severe lameness. A small horizontal crack might become visible in the coronet. Sometimes it only becomes visible after the pasterns are trimmed in a show clip. If the horse has light-colored hooves, telltale discoloration of the hoof or in the white line is a warning sign as are distended veins in the pastern and fetlock, and an increased digital pulse. Some horses present no symptoms at all except lameness. Riders should look for subtle signs when they ride, including a shortened or uneven stride, reticence to change leads, and refusal to jump.

Prevention tip: Keep the horse on a frequent shoeing schedule. Avoid flares in the hoof wall and any overgrowth in the toe that causes stretching in the white line. Inspect the feet daily for signs of heat, swelling, and cracks. Don't just look at them, feel them with your hands, and learn what the normal temperature is and what areas are normally hard or soft to touch.

Treatment: At the first sign of abscess, check the horse's tetanus status, and arrange for a booster shot if needed. Your farrier or veterinarian will use hoof testers to find the exact source of the pain, which may or may not be the inflamed area. Be sure that the abscess is completely drained and treated before returning the horse to use, since an abscess can cause permanent damage if allowed to fester inside the foot. The drainage track will need to be flushed and medicated. You may be asked to soak the foot daily, usually in Epsom salts.

Your veterinarian might give you medications for the horse designed to relieve pain, reduce the swelling, and fight off the infection.

The foot will need to be wrapped with gauze pads and vet wrap or kept in a clean medication boot with gauze pads covering the drainage point. In the second phase of treatment, the horse will probably need to be shod with a full plastic pad under a regular shoe or be fitted with a removable hospital plate.

ANGULAR LIMB DEFORMITIES

The equine foot is a wonderful mechanism. A hoof acts as an adjustable stabilizer at the end of each leg. As the weight and force moves downward through bones and other structures of the leg, the foot adjusts by growing more heel, or more hoof wall toward the inside or outside. Each growth spurt is an adjustment designed to create a support platform.

A well-conformed horse usually has well-conformed feet. The rest of our horses are less than perfect. Some are far from perfect. Their conformation creates leg and foot problems such as toe-in, toe-out, knock-knees, bow-legs, and cow hocks.

Abnormal development of the leg bones, abnormal lower-leg structures, and the foot's attempts to compensate for them are lumped together in a category called "angular limb deformities." The term falls under the broader topic of developmental orthopedic diseases.

An angular limb deformity can be as common as the "back at the knee" conformation found in many Thoroughbreds.

Most people think that angular limb deformities are congenital problems present in young foals at birth, but mature horses can acquire limb deformities, too, particularly as an after-effect of a traumatic injury.

Sometimes, foals are born with uneven or twisted limbs, but if their upper body conformation is correct, the normal weight-bearing process down the limb becomes a self-adjusting mechanism. As the foal starts to exercise, its feet and lower legs will grow and the unevenness often goes away over time.

To learn more about angular limb problems, study the anatomy of the equine knee, fetlock, and hock. Familiarize yourself with the developmental time frame for the leg bones of a horse. Problems can be categorized in

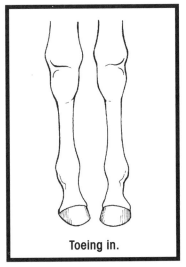

Toeing in.

two groups: 1) uneven growth (one side of a bone grows faster than the other side, which makes the "stacking" of bones uneven); and 2) abnormal alignment of the bones in a joint resulting in the rotation of the limb. Such angular deformities don't line up when you face the foal. Rotational deformities might line up, but the limb is not facing in the same direction as the head of the horse!

In a foal with good conformation, when you look at it head on, you can imagine a straight, vertical line running from its shoulder

Toeing out.

down through its knee, lower leg, and center of the hoof.

If you are considering buying a horse with any type of angular limb deformity, proceed with caution. These horses are high maintenance and are prone to injury. Often, their gaits will be choppy, inefficient, and uncomfortable for a rider. Such a horse might have limited potential unless it is always ridden by a light-weight rider.

If you already have a horse with abnormal conformation, one that is toed-in or toed-out for example, pay attention to how it is trimmed or shod so you'll learn what makes it most comfortable. It might be helpful to examine the horse's worn shoes when the farrier pulls them. The shoes will give you clues to how the horse is landing and bearing its weight. It may be difficult to trim the feet of a horse with an angular deformity so that it lands flat. Its coronary band often will be distorted, too.

It is not unusual for horses with angular limb deformities to develop sidebone or low ringbone early in life.

Prevention: Avoid bloodlines with congenital abnormal conformation. Treat all foal injuries as potentially life threatening, and monitor their recovery carefully. Have foals examined (not necessarily trimmed) regularly by a veterinarian and a farrier. If the foal's legs are developing unevenly, seek treatment early. Learn all you can about the horse's leg.

Warning signs: Sometimes, the foal's problem is not recognized by the owner until the hoof starts to look abnormal or the coronary band appears to be distorted. The foal can develop sheared heels, or the bottom of the foot may show that the frog seems to point at an angle, instead of straight ahead.

All of these are big red flags of warning to the owner, indicating that the foal needs to be carefully examined by an experienced farrier and veterinarian. Sometimes, both of the foal's front legs will be affected; at other times, it may be just one leg.

Some amount of "toe out" conformation is normal in the hind feet of adult horses.

Treatment: Treatment of angular limb deformities can range from conservative approaches such as splinting or bandaging legs to complex high-tech surgical interventions. For some leg problems, surgery has become a common solution.

Normal procedures for more foals include a physical examination and taking radiographs of the leg. It might be helpful if you have a clear profile, head on, and end on photos of the dam and sire of the foal to show your veterinarian. You might hear the words "valgus" and "varus" in the diagnosis, which mean simply "out" and "in" in respect to the leg below a specific joint. For example, "fetlock varus" simply means toeing in. The terms might sound complicated, but the veterinarian needs them to identify and classify the angulation of the different joints, since a deformity in one is usually compensated for in the joint below it.

As a memory aid, I remember that valgus means "out" by the simple means of it having more letters than varus; out also has more letters than in. When someone says that a horse has "carpus valgus" problems, I visualize a knee, with the leg below it going "out"…and by thinking of the horse's two front legs, "knock-kneed" is the final picture I get.

"Carpus varus" would mean the cannon bone heads inward, i.e. bow-legged stance. Likewise, "fetlock varus" would send the pastern inward, giving a horse the "toe in" stance. "Fetlock valgus" would send the pastern outward, so the foot would toe out. Remember that the source of the problem is not in the bone that is out of alignment, but with the joint above it.

Conservative intervention could begin with splints bandaged onto the leg, or with glue-on shoes that have little shelves on the inside or outside of the hoof wall. These shelves, called medial (inside) or lateral (outside) extensions create a loading surface that redirects weight and force descending through the leg.

Minor surgery to equalize growth often gives excellent results and many foals go on to successful athletic careers. Other foals can be improved, but will always bear a characteristic abnormal stance that can affect their performance and their value. Still others cannot be helped by surgery, but they still might be usable horses if given proper hoofcare and therapy throughout their lives.

ATROPHIED FROG

An atrophied, or shrunken, frog is usually found in horses with contracted heels. Which comes first? No one seems to know. Often frog atrophy is seen in horses with navicular lameness, since they deliberately avoid bearing weight on the posterior part of their feet. Hence, circulation is affected, the role of the frog is altered, and the frog — possibly along with its digital cushion — loses mass, and shrinks up into the foot. One of the most perplexing instances of frog atrophy is in the flat-footed horse. One would think that the frog of a flat-footed horse would grow larger. Sometimes the frogs do, but in other horses, the atrophied frog loses its distinction from the rest of the foot.

Some horses have deviant hoof conformation all their adult lives; others develop it as a compensatory reaction to injury, pain, or uneven weight-bearing problems. If you believe that your horse's frog is shrinking, consult both your farrier and veterinarian about the problem. It should be noticeable if you've been cleaning your horse's feet regularly. If such a problem develops, consider leaving your horse barefoot for a period of time and have it trimmed frequently with nice short toes. If contracted heels are a problem, treat both the heels and the frog.

Your veterinarian might take radiographs to show ossification in the collateral cartilages, which is often a predisposing factor leading to atrophied frogs and contracted heels. Both problems develop as the horse shifts its weight, rocking back and forth, seeking a more comfortable place to land and stand on badly misshapen feet. Upright pasterns may predispose a horse to any or all of these problems. As the horse's atrophied frogs and contracted heels get worse, its pasterns may become more upright as a result of its abnormal stance (see also the section on contracted heels).

BRIDLE LAMENESS

Bridle lameness is not a specific type of lameness. Bridle

lameness means that a horse shows no signs of unsoundness when at liberty, or perhaps when it is exercised on a long line. However, under tack with a rider, the horse might be unable to perform certain movements. It might resist changing leads, or refuse jumps. Sometimes, the cause is simply ill-fitting tack, overbridling, inappropriate tack, or poorly fitting boots. Sometimes a horse with bridle lameness will go sound if a lighter-weight, or more expert rider is substituted for its normal rider.

Riders often complain to farriers about their horses stumbling or refusing leads. There is not much farriers can do to correct cases of bridle lameness since shoeing usually has no effect on the problem.

Treatment: If the horse has intermittent lameness problems that might be attributed to bridle lameness, its rider should work with a trainer to make sure that the rider is in balance and is not adding to the horse's problem. All of the horse's tack should be carefully checked along with examining how it fits both the horse and rider. Riders should not expect farriers and veterinarians to evaluate tack selection or fit.

If your horse has developed bridle lameness, arrange to have your farrier and veterinarian watch as the horse is first worked without tack, and then tack it up and ride it while they watch. Sometimes a farrier can make minor adjustments in the shoes' breakover to decrease the effort the horse puts into each stride.

BRUISING

Many experts consider bruising to be the most common lameness problem experienced by pleasure horses in America today. The experts say there are thousands of thin-walled, thin-soled, flat-footed horses with chronic bruising problems. Other experts think that bruising is over-diagnosed and that horses should not be lame from normal use. Horses with similar hoof conformation might have completely different reactions to the same trauma to their hooves. Horses have different thresholds of pain, and some are simply tender-footed.

Bruising can occur at the coronet, inside the wall, under the sole, at the white line, and at the heels. A bruise is difficult to isolate as a cause for pain or loss of performance in a horse, because a bruise is evidence of a past trauma that may or may not be causing the horse pain currently.

Coronet bruising

Trauma to the coronet can cause a bruise to form in that area. On a horse with white feet, you might see a swollen area on the coronet, followed a few weeks later by a red or purple area growing down the hoof wall. By the time you see the bruise, it probably has healed completely at the source of the injury. Horses that forge and interfere often show bruising; driving and draft horses or horses shod with permanent studs who step on themselves also can have this problem. Bell boots or over-reach boots are one way to protect the tender coronet area of horses prone to interference.

Heel bruising (corns)

Take a look at a shoe that has been pulled off a horse. On the side that is nailed to the foot, notice the heel area. Can you see what looks like scrape marks worn into the steel? Those are heel wear marks, caused by the expansion and contraction of the hoof capsule as it bears the horse's weight. Any sort of abnormal pressure, such as unequal pressure between the two heels of the same foot, a loose shoe, or nailing the shoe to an unlevel foot will cause the bearing point of the heels (called "seat of corn") to be injured. Sometimes called a "corn," the injury is a bruise. It can become infected if left untreated and will cause lameness. Heel bruises are one of the most common causes of minor lameness in horses, and are almost always caused by neglect.

The most common cause of a corn is shoes that are left on too long. Other causes are shoes that are too short in the heels or too small all over for the foot. A rivet, used to hold a pad onto a shoe, could also dig into the heel area and cause a corn. A completely avoidable cause of heel bruises is screwing studs too deeply into their holes and damaging the heel area. Corns are common in horses with underrun heels or contracted heels.

Heel bruises will stop causing the horse pain once the horseshoe has been removed, unless infection has set in. In that case, the bruise is treated like an abscess.

Sole bruising (subsolar bruising)

The horse's sole has both an insensitive (outer) sole and a sensitive inner sole. The sensitive sole has a corium, a vast web of tiny blood vessels. If the outer sole is thin, or the foot is flat, the sensitive sole is vulnerable to sharp objects or bruising from the constant compression of the foot against a hard, unforgiving surface. When the blood vessels are damaged, they leak, then a bruise forms under the sole. The horse may or may not go lame.

Ordinarily, an injury like this would become inflamed and swell, but inside the unforgiving horn of the sole, when a bruise forms between the coffin bone and the horny sole, there is no room for the bruised area to swell without displacing the coffin bone. When the farrier trims the insensitive sole at the next shoeing, he or she will see yellow or purple blotches on the fresh sole. On a dark-footed horse, these bruises aren't always visible.

A horse owner is often horrified looking over the farrier's shoulder and seeing a bruise in the new sole. In most cases, this bruising is evidence of an insult that has come and gone, and is no longer causing the horse pain.

An exception to this would be a semi-circular bruise around the point of the frog. This might be an indication of downward pressure of the coffin bone against the solar corium. It is commonly seen in club-footed and laminitic horses, especially road foundered horses that have been ridden hard on paved roads without proper hoof protection. Chronic pawers also might show this type of a bruise, or white line staining. Such horses should be kept shod to protect the toes.

Some people use the term "stone bruise" in all cases where there is sole bruising and pain in the sole, but that is a misnomer. In most of those cases, the horse did not accidentally step on a sharp stone. If your horse has a sole bruising problem, it is probably because of his foot condition and conformation, or the environment he is worked on (soft, wet feet working on a hard surface are damaged easily).

Always consult your veterinarian if the lameness persists. Give the horse a few days off, with some extra time after the pain subsides to make sure healing is complete. If the lameness persists, the problem is probably not a bruise in the sole.

Make sure that you clean out the concave area under your horse's shoe each day, so that there is no matter caught there putting pressure on the sole. Consider getting your farrier to put plastic or leather pads under your horse's shoes as a temporary treatment.

If the horse is lame, your veterinarian might prescribe medication. Check the horse's stall and make sure that it is not standing on concrete. Iincrease the depth of its bedding, and wall up the edges of the stall to keep the bedding from dispersing. Hoof hardening products might help toughen up the soles of your horse's feet. Ask your farrier about new ideas for treating flat feet or thin soles. New products are introduced all the time. One might help your horse.

Wall bruising (submural hoof tearing)

This problem is difficult to see in a dark foot, difficult to pinpoint as a source of pain if a bruise is seen, and has no real treatment other than rest. It often is associated with horses that have thin hoof walls and weak feet, and indicates that some sort of laminar insult has injured the coffin bone-hoof wall tissues. Wall bruises are generally an indication of inferior foot condition rather than a cause of lameness. Horses that have wall bruises often have problems with solar bruises as well. Wall bruises often are confused with abscesses in the hoof wall, and what might appear to be a bruise under the wall, visible on a thin-walled horse, is probably the evidence of a former injury or a coronet bruise growing down the hoof.

It is not unusual for a light-colored hoof wall to show bruising when a farrier rasps off a flare. The thinned wall might have been stretched or damaged as a result of the flare. Horses that are chronic stall kickers are thought to suffer from lameness due to wall bruising, but it is difficult to document. Hoof walls on flat-footed draft horses with deliberately created lateral flares are excellent museums of hoof wall bruises.

Another sign of laminar damage is blood in the white zone, the light-colored area at the inner perimeter of the foot where the hoof wall meets the sole. This is evidence of a trauma to the laminae, but the insult is long past by the time it becomes visible in the newly trimmed wall.

Blood staining at the white line should not be confused with blood caused by nailing injuries during shoeing or with the half-moon bruise of pressure from the coffin bone, which would be between the white line and the point of the frog. Horses that have dramatic correction done to rebalance their feet often show blood at the white line, probably caused by bending of the hoof wall from excess flares or toe length.

Prevention: The best way to avoid wall weakness is to feed a good-quality hoof-growth supplement daily, maintain a frequent shoeing schedule, and avoid over-long toes and flares. Protective bell boots could help horses wearing toe grabs when they aren't competing. Glue-on shoes are an excellent option for horses prone to wall problems.

CANKER

Canker is a mess. It looks like someone poured acid on the frog, and the tissue has exploded. Canker is often mistaken for a really bad case of thrush. The difference is that canker is a type of hyperplasia, an excessive growth of the cells. This abnormal frog tissue, or vegetative growth, is characterized by an oozing, cottage cheese-like substance and an extremely foul odor.

Prevention: Canker is associated with hot, humid climates, neglect of hoofcare, and unsanitary stabling. I receive inquiries about new treatments for canker from farriers in southeastern Asia and Africa, where it is still common. In North America, the few cases seen are often in draft breeds, and it is seen more often in hind limbs than front limbs.

Treatment: Canker is a veterinary problem. Your horse will require both debridement of hoof tissue (usually from the sole and frog) and daily medication over a period of time. The foot must be cleaned repeatedly. Before the medication is put on topically, any loose horn is removed and the affected area is scrubbed with Betadine. Then the sole is packed with gauze soaked in a strong astringent such as picric acid. (The astringent stings, so watch out for your own safety as the horse starts dancing around.) You will need to keep its foot cleaned and wrapped. After you are done, use duct tape to cover the foot.

CIRCULATION (BLOOD FLOW) TO THE EQUINE FOOT

A complex blood supply constantly fills and drains the horse's foot. A major artery descends through the leg, splits in two, and descends into the foot, where the two branches of the main descending artery are rejoined in an important juncture tucked inside the coffin bone called "the terminal arch." Branches of the terminal arch poke through the coffin bone and emerge around its circumference, forming a ring, providing a good blood supply around the foot called "the circumflex artery."

If you could see a diagram of the blood supply to the foot, it would look like two rings arranged in a double-decker affair. The circumflex artery travels around the circumference of the coffin bone, creating a "ground floor" blood supply, while a second orbital blood supply travels through the coronary band, forming the "second story" blood supply.

The coffin bone has many tiny holes in it. Each one acts as a conduit for a tiny artery whose purpose is to supply blood to the laminae, the Velcro-like fibers that link the coffin bone to the hoof wall, which has no blood supply at this level. The sole has a corium which holds a bed of tiny blood vessels. This is where the blood usually comes from if a horse is "pricked" during shoeing or steps on a nail.

One of the most serious aspects of horse shoeing is that a horse with a thin sole has inadequate protection for the sensitive structures of the foot. This problem is found in all breeds, but is particularly troublesome in Thoroughbred racehorses. A classic example is a flat-footed horse that is shod with a wide-web shoe. If the shoe is wide enough and the sole thin enough, the circumflex artery can be pinched.

Major injuries to the blood supply in the foot are rare, but sometimes freak accidents cut off circulation. For example, when a horse gets its foot caught in wire, it can have a tourniquet effect on the horse's lower leg, cutting off circulation.

Laminitis is the most common disease associated with the circulation of blood through the foot. How the disease works is not known for certain. The bond between inside and outside laminae is broken, perhaps due to an interruption or because of the toxic agents in the blood supply, and the coffin bone becomes unstable in the foot. Laminae cannot reattach, so a new hoof wall must grow down from the coronary band.

Healthy hooves require a healthy blood supply. Hoof growth is dependent on a healthy coronary band. Ordinary walking and pasture activity plus equal weight bearing in the hoof's structures are important for a horse to keep the blood supply in good working order and promote growth.

COFFIN JOINT DEGENERATION
(CHRONIC HOOF PAIN, HOOF CAPSULE DISEASE)

Many athletic horses are routinely treated for nonspecific coffin joint lameness. Owners find the vagueness of the diagnosis frustrating, but they usually are pleased when their horses' overall soundness improves following treatment.

Coffin joint degeneration is a collective name for visible and invisible "wear and tear" inside the coffin joint. Veterinarians sometimes describe it as an "arthritis-like" condition in the joint. The joint is made up of three bones: coffin bone, short pastern bone, and navicular bone. The coffin joint is a complex junction, where the constant stress of weight bearing and flexion take their toll.

Veterinarians take radiographs to check for signs of degeneration in the coffin joint. Treatment options are limited. Since the joint is inside the hoof capsule, it can't be manipulated as easily as other joints. Surgery is difficult in this area.

Prevention: To prevent or slow down coffin bone degeneration, use good sense in training and working your horse. Avoid excessively hard surfaces and long work sessions. Make sure the horse's shoes fit, that the shoeing is done right, and is done on a regular schedule. Cool your horse off properly after work. With older or advanced-level horses, work with your trainer, farrier, and vet to be sensitive to any signs that might signal changes occurring inside the foot.

Warning signs: Intermittent or continuing lameness has several causes. Coffin-joint degeneration is one of them.

Symptoms of this hoof capsule disease include an uneven gait, a shortened stride, stumbling, frequent change of leads, refusal to change leads, and refusal to jump. A common warning sign expressed by the rider might be summed up in one sentence, "My horse isn't going right."

Treatment: The most common treatment is a combination of "creative" shoeing to try to make the horse more comfortable (pads, bar shoes, wider shoes, clips — or a custom-made shoe) and medication for pain management. Many veterinarians recommend a series of injections of polysulfated gly-cosaminoglycans (PSAGs), which is basically like changing the oil in the joint. Corticosteroids are sometimes used alone or in combination with PSAGs.

Neurectomy is a last resort treatment. The surgeon severs one or more nerves in the horse's foot so it can't feel pain. It also can't feel anything else in the part of the foot that has been desensitized. "Nerved" horses need careful management and frequent foot examinations. They can end up with a street nail, or other puncture wound, and never even feel it.

CONTRACTED HEELS, SHEARED HEELS

Contracted heels are usually seen in a foot with a shriveled up frog. Nobody knows which problem starts first.

Contracted heels mean that the foot is trying to change its shape to relieve discomfort, either while weight bearing or when landing in each stride. Structures inside the foot begin collapsing or grating up against another structure. Meanwhile, the hoof capsule adjusts by changing its shape.

Horses with sidebones often have contracted heels as well. If the horse avoids putting weight on its heels, the posterior part of the foot will cease to function properly and will lose its normal circulation.

A foot might have one or both heels in a contracted state. When only one heel is affected, the horse usually is said to have "sheared heels." This can be a minor blemish, or a major cause of lameness, depending on severity and duration of the condition.

Viewed from behind, a sheared heel foot looks uneven. One heel bulb will be a high lump at the hairline, while the other will look underrun, and have a hairline close to the ground.

Sheared heels are difficult to correct. It's a chronic problem in many jumping horses. Often a deep sulcus forms between the bulbs of the heels, and the foot literally "shears" with each step the horse takes. The heels move independently of one another, instead of in unison. One heel lands before the other at each stride.

Sheared heels can be caused by uneven landing, which in turn can be caused by some source of pain in the foot or leg, so that the horse compensates for the lameness which ends up damaging the heels. Sheared heels also can be inadvertently caused by poor shoeing. For example, the farrier may try to correct faulty foot conformation for a horse going into a halter class, or try to correct gait faults by "jacking the foot" until it lands flat. "Cranking on the hoof capsule" (lowering one side more than another) usually creates a level-landing foot for only a short time after the trimming. Then the foot, like water, seeks its own level by growing hoof horn which puts the foot almost instantly out of balance.

It is not unusual for sheared heels to become infected with thrush and to bleed. Contracted heels also become infected with thrush.

Prevention: Regular foot care and attention to hoof conformation will assure that the horse is bearing weight normally. Signs of the heels starting to contract should be taken as a warning that something is going wrong in the foot.

Warning signs: The following problems may precede sheared heels or contracted heels: a change in the angle of the coronet, shrinking of the frog, foot soreness after working on hard surfaces, exaggerated heel growth, heels curling inward, and uneven heel bulbs (when viewed from behind).

Treatment: Expert farrier care will be needed to get the foot level and shod with a shoe that will protect and support the foot with sheared or contracted heels. Egg bar shoes are used on horses that must be kept in training.

If a horse can be laid up, simply pulling the shoes and leveling the foot might be all that is needed to correct the problem. Sometimes, the farrier will "float" affected parts of the foot. If the horse's bare foot can be wrapped in moist towels, or put in a water boot, the floated section soon will seem to sink to the ground. What is really happening is that the coronet is relaxing and returning to its normal position. As the jammed portion comes down to the ground, the horse should begin to bear weight normally again. The farrier should check the horse again in a few days.

Many horses have permanent structural damage to their feet from sheared heels. The deep crease between their heels is a permanent fissure in the hoof capsule's integrity. Such horses require some sort of support bar shoe for athletic use.

CORONARY BAND AND CORONET

"Coronet" and "coronary band" are two terms that are often used interchangeably, although they are two separate structures. I use a little word association to keep the two separate. I think of the coronet as the "crown" of the hoof. Underneath the coronet lies the coronary band, which contains the blood supply necessary to "feed" all the new cells growing in the hoof wall. I can associate "coronet" with "crown" and "coronary" with "from the heart," and keep the two structures — and names — separate.

To continue with word association, think of the coronary band as a bracelet carrying the blood supply. It surrounds the top of the hoof wall (epidermis), which has hair-like papilla, or plug-like units, that interlock with the coronary groove's own papilla. As long as they are meshed together, they receive the nutrients and oxygen they need from the blood supply in the coronary band and the hoof wall can grow downward. On the inside, the dermis of the coronet, a similar system nourishes the inner hoof wall's laminae, which interlock with the laminae attached to the coffin bone.

Visualizing these interlocking parts attaching as Velcro does is one of the best analogies I can use to discuss the structures inside an equine foot. Velcro is a recently invented product widely used as a fastener. Usually, one Velcro strip carries tiny hook-like parts made to imitate the burrs on a thistle, while the matching Velcro strip has soft, springy fibers the "burrs" will readily stick to when the two strips are pressed together.

While the horny hoof wall contains no bone and has no direct blood supply, it can be said that it is attached like Velcro to the coffin bone by the laminae and again to the coronet by the papilla. Oddly enough, if you dissect a foot and pull the inner and outer hoof apart, there is a little sound much like the sound Velcro makes when its two parts are separated.

Remember how you were advised to brush the coronet each day? It might be valuable, particularly for a stall-bound horse, to be massaged at the coronet or hosed off with running water sprayed on the coronet to stimulate blood supply in the upper region of the foot. Both techniques help to ensure that nutrients are getting to the hoof wall. If you are feeding your horse an expensive hoof-growth supplement, you know how important it is for the body to be able to absorb the nutrients. A coronet that has been bruised or is recovering from a laceration takes a long time to regenerate healthy tissue, and needs all the help it can get.

CORONARY BAND JAMMING

The coronet should look like a nice, straight line of even height. It should have a very slight hardness to the touch under the skin and hair. It should curve down slightly at the heels. If the horse is having trouble with imbalance in its movement or uneven hoof wall growth, the coronet might have been "jammed." If so, there will be a raised, hairless area at the coronet, usually at the quarters, where the hoof wall curves. Farriers have different ways of describing what causes jamming: some will say that a section of the foot grows faster than others, forcing the coronet to be pushed upward (for more information, see the section on flares in the hoof wall).

A more severe type of coronary band jamming is a side effect of laminitis and chronic founder (see the description of laminitis in Chapter 4). Since the most common area of damage to the laminae is in the toe region, the heels often appear to grow more quickly than the toe. The coronet becomes parallel to the ground and may even curve upward at the heels. Once the corium of the coronary band has been compressed, it compromises the important blood supply to the toe area, compounding the effect of the high heels.

Warning signs: If the hairline over the coronet looks like it has a bump in it, or if the hair stick outs and does not lie flat on the hoof, you need to check for coronet jamming.

Here's a prevention tip: Shorten the time between shoeing appointments so that flares will not occur.

Treatment: Your farrier will automatically take

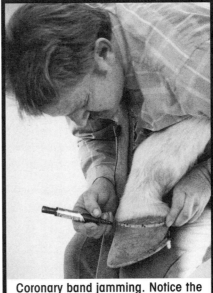

Coronary band jamming. Notice the curved appearance.

care of flares in the trimming process, or rasp off the flared area after the shoe is in place. If you watch closely, you will see the coronary band relax after the pressure is released.

To ease the pain of a horse with upright, high-heeled, foundered feet, your farrier or veterinarian might suggest a full or partial toe resection (i.e., the removal of the hoof wall to relieve pressure on the coronary band) or a relatively new technique in which a groove is cut in the hoof wall parallel to the coronary band, just below the periople. This technique is called "dorsal wall grooving" or "horizontal resectioning."

CORONARY BAND SWELLING AND LESIONS

A puffy, swollen coronary band is a warning sign that a major problem is developing. Localized swelling at one point on the coronary band is an initial warning sign that an infection inside the foot is looking for a way out. Generalized swelling and lesions along the coronary band are symptoms of vesicular stomatitis virus (VSV), a highly contagious and deadly disease in horses. VSV is rarely seen in the United States outside the southwestern states. In some cases, the swelling can produce small blisters that will burst and expose raw tissue.

If you suspect that the horse has VSV, do not touch the infected area. Call your veterinarian immediately. Isolate the horse from other animals and do not put a new horse in the infected horse's stall. Wear gloves whenever you care for the horse. VSV can be transmitted to humans from animals.

CUSHING'S DISEASE (Cushing's Syndrome, Cushingoid horse, Cushingoid laminitis, Cushingoid Disease, Pituitary Adenoma)

Horses suffering from Cushing's disease really stand out in the herd. They are usually older horses that have long, shaggy coats no matter what the season. Such horses might never shed out in warm weather. They crave drinking water, sweat profusely, and usually become painfully thin. Cushing sufferers are prone to frequent, and sometimes unpredictable, bouts of chronic laminitis and hoof abscesses. The cause of all these symptoms is a tumor in the pituitary gland in the brain.

Prevention: No one really knows how a tumor in the brain can cause laminitis and abscesses in the feet. Your veterinarian might take blood and urine tests to investigate whether or not it is likely that Cushing's disease is the problem. Remember that many older ponies are prone to chronic founder but do not have a pituitary tumor.

The best treatment for the laminitis part of Cushing's disease is to plan a preventive program of frequent hoofcare. Keep the feet trimmed and level, assuring a good, strong bond between the hoof wall and coffin bone. Your veterinarian may also suggest dietary changes and pain management through drug therapy. Keep the horse off lush pasture and away from rich sweet feed.

Keeping the horse shod with frog-support shoes, such as

heart bars that are properly fit, may help keep the horse more comfortable.

Warning signs: All the classic signs of laminitis — feet "nailed to the ground," hind legs camped far forward beneath the body, strong digital pulse, heat in the feet — will indicate the horse is foundering. Laminitis is an almost inevitable result of Cushing's disease. (Laminitis, or chronic founder, also has many other causes.)

Treatment: Consult your veterinarian immediately when signs of laminitis begin and do what you can to keep the horse comfortable. Consider clipping the horse. You may be able to try different drugs or feed supplements to see if there is an effect, but at this time there is no known cure or treatment for this problem. Treat abscesses if they develop. They are a secondary effect of the laminitis.

FLAT FEET

Are horses born with flat feet or are such feet created? Like many of the other problems described in this chapter, flat feet are thought to be a man-made problem, due to poor care (by improper shoeing and trimming the horse at a young age or working it too hard on poor surfaces) or due to the selection process on the part of breeders (who ignore the value of good feet, soundness, and longevity of athleticism).

The foot is the great equalizer of the horse's conformation. Nature tells the foot to grow longer, grow forward, grow more heel, etc. to carry the load of the horse's body and head. Sometimes, the foot just isn't in shape to carry the load.

Flat feet are exposed to bruising with every step a horse takes. Horses with this problem might be chronically footsore and attempts to increase concavity in the sole could make the horse even more sensitive.

Farriers and veterinarians often talk about "dropped" soles, which is a change in the sole, and is very different from (and much more serious than) "normal" flat feet seen in many of the English-riding breeds.

The important consideration in a flat foot is how thick the sole is (i.e,. how much tissue is between the ground and the sensitive sole, and between it and the coffin bone). Sometimes, horses can have a false sole, or double sole.

Flat-footed horses generally have a difficult time recovering from laminitis. Also, many foundered horses develop flat feet as a consequence of their ordeal. Some farriers believe that overweight horses, particularly young horses, develop flat feet.

To further complicate the flat foot, you should know that the ground surface of the coffin bone is not normally parallel to the ground. It is normally suspended at an angle of six to 10 degrees above parallel; you will notice that in a typical lateral radiograph if you draw a line representing the ground, then trace the ground surface of the coffin bone. In many flat feet, the coffin bone will be parallel to the ground, putting more strain on the deep digital flexor tendon.

Prevention: This is a tough condition to prevent, particularly if the horse lives in a wet environment or has Thoroughbred or northern European breeding. Horses in wet, low countries (Ireland, England, France, The Netherlands, etc.) often have extremely broad-toed, pancake-like feet as part of their normal conformation. Clydesdales and Shires are extreme examples. Their terrain is often wet and they were bred to plow through thick mud. The foot of a Clydesdale or Shire bears weight differently than the foot of, say, an Arabian or Andalusian who moves naturally above the ground, not through it.

Consider keeping flat-footed horses stabled in deep bedding, particularly if concrete is at the bottom of the stall. If you have any British or Irish trainers or barn managers in your area, ask them to explain to you what a "deep litter bed" is, and if they recommend that you try it.

If you have radiographs of your horse's flat feet, ask a veterinarian to look at them and show you how much (or how little) sole cushioning is under the coffin bone. To prevent lameness, pick the feet out often and don't let anything get trapped under the bevels of the shoes. If your pasture is rocky or hard, consider turning the horse out in an indoor arena or sand ring.

Warning signs: Lack of concavity, frequent bruising, foot-sore, and going gimpy are all warning signs. A semi-circular bruise between the toe and point of frog is a serious cause for alarm because it indicates compression and bruising along the perimeter of the coffin bone (see bruising section).

Treatment: Your farrier probably deals with flat-footed horses every day. These are management-intensive horses. Be careful where you work a flat-footed horse. It will do better on soft going rather than going on a paved road, or even a tar or gravel surface. Frog support shoes are popular options to try on a flat-footed horse. The shoes are thought to enhance circulation throughout the foot. All shoes should be reverse-beveled at the inside rim ground surface to mini-mize sole pressure. The farrier will use a rasp to do this or will shape the shoe with a grinder. If you see any sign of bruising or discomfort soon after shoeing, notify your farrier so that the shoes can be replaced or adjusted.

Pads might be helpful to some horses, but farriers some-times advise against putting pads on flat-footed horses because the horses seem to become "pad-dependent" and will be footsore without the pads. Sometimes, the foot will flatten even more, or the frog will change. Remember that the pad traps moisture under it, which is not good for even a healthy sole. It is difficult to get much packing under a pad on a flat foot. Remember that a full pad hides the sole from view, so if an abscess develops, you might not be aware of it as quickly as you would with an unpadded foot. You might prefer to shoe with pads when the horse needs them for re-covery from a bruise or abscess, rather than as standard equipment, put on with every shoeing.

Rim pads are a quick, temporary aid for flat feet, as they increase the space between the foot and the shoe, lifting the exposed sole a centimeter or so from the ground. They usually flatten quickly, though. They can be used in conjunction with full pads to create space where packing can be used.

Egg bar shoes work on some flat-footed horses, but the shoe width is a consideration, since you do not want any pressure on the sole. Farriers hate to be called back to see a flat-footed horse who has "fallen through" its new egg bar shoes and has sole pressure bruises. What do you try next? Going barefoot?

Artificially creating a concave foot with a knife is risky on a flat foot, even though it is routinely done to many racehorses before they race. Remember that most racehorses are young, and their feet are strong. Perhaps many of the problems we see with former racehorses is a result of pre-race "doming," which is thought to create a "cup" effect and propel the horse forward. The resulting dome effect usually won't last long, and if the sole is thin, the coffin bone will be even more susceptible to bruising.

Various home remedies and over-the-counter hoofcare products are used on flat-footed horses. Ask racetrack grooms in your area what they use for stinging feet. If you live in a wet climate, consider "hoof hardener" products that you paint onto the bottom of the feet. A hoof hardener is designed to dry out the sole and encourage growth of a thicker sole.

FLEXURAL DEFORMITIES ("CLUB FOOT")

Many problems in the upper limb are expressed through the foot. One of the most obvious is a "club foot" on a horse. A club foot is the visible outward effect of a flexural deformity. "Flexural" structures in the horse are the spring-like tendons that lift and bend the leg. As with most problems, the tendon deformity may be present at birth (congenital) or might appear later in the foal's development (acquired).

Three main tendons run down the horse's leg. All three ultimately attach in or near the foot. Disruption of normal growth or function of one, two, or even all three of these tendons will result in a foot being pulled in an unnatural direction, both by the tendon as it works to lift and flex the leg, and in the way the foot travels through the air and lands.

Flexural deformities are not very well-understood. No one is really sure what causes them, although some sort of response to pain seems to be at their root. In simple terms: If a muscle hurts, it will not relax. It will be tense, and the tendon running down the leg might be tense all the way to the foot. In the tensed position, the tendon might hold

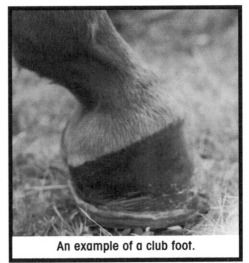

An example of a club foot.

the coffin bone in an abnormal angle to the ground, or the horse might bear weight differently. If the condition persists, the adaptable horse once again tries to compensate, by building up the hoof to ease the stress. If the pain is up the back of the pastern and caused by the deep digital flexor tendon, the horse's foot might grow exaggerated heels. At some point, the condition may be irreversible.

Many myths and lots of unreliable information in the horse industry have misinformed horse owners about club feet. The problem is extremely common in some breeds. Breeders are defensive about referring to club feet as a deformity. Some people still believe that the tendon is "contracted," although it is physically impossible for a tendon to contract. Club feet are thought to be an inherited characteristic, although cases can develop through poor management and environmental factors. Club feet are not caused by the bones growing faster than the tendons.

In a foal, club foot is a manageable problem, especially if it is treated soon after the onset of the problem. Existing club feet in adult horses may or may not be manageable. In an adult horse, club feet are rarely, if ever, reversible.

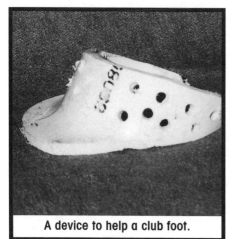

A device to help a club foot.

Complications of the club foot include chronic lameness, collapse of the opposite foot, and even mechanical laminitis, or rotation of the coffin bone so that the laminae-hoof wall bond is ripped.

The opposite of a tight tendon is a "lax" tendon. It is a problem found in newborn foals. The Clydesdale breed is particularly susceptible to this problem. The pasterns appear to be almost horizontal to the ground. Most foals quickly recover. Tendon laxity may also be a temporary problem after a leg cast or brace is removed.

Prevention: Notify your veterinarian and farrier of any injury to foals. Keep photographic records of your horses' feet to compare any suspect changes. If a horse is laid up, find ways for the horse to get exercise, either by swimming or regular massage and stretching exercises. Monitor the diets of foals very carefully.

Warning signs: Change in the pastern angle (fetlock seems to be moving up and forward), growth of excess heel, abnormal growth rings in the hoof wall, leveling of the coronary band, dish in the front of the hoof wall. The horse might appear to be knuckling over at the pastern or fetlock, or the pastern might drop and the horse begins to walk on the bulbs of its heels, with the toe not bearing any weight. In some cases, the horse might bear weight only on the toe, popularly called "ballerina syndrome." One or both front feet might be affected. Adult horses might acquire a club foot following an injury.

Treatment: Conservative treatment begins with bandaging and splints and toe or heel "extension" shoes that redirect stress or provide extra support for weak structures. Medication therapy might be helpful as well.

More radical treatment involves surgery, probably followed by corrective shoes.

Hoof trimming techniques are sometimes helpful in visually correcting mildly deformed feet, but the effect is usually helpful for cosmetic purposes only and the foot will soon return to its clubby appearance if left untrimmed.

Extension shoes and built-up heels may be helpful to some horses. If you don't think they look very pretty, your farrier can disguise the shoes using a hoof-repair compound so that the horse will not pull them off and the foot will appear normal.

GAIT INTERFERENCE INJURIES

Does your horse always seem to have minor cuts and scrapes on its heel bulbs or around the coronet? Do you hear a clinking sound whenever you ride on a hard surface? Does your horse pull shoes off frequently?

Horses with gait interference problems commonly injure their front feet. Usually, a hind foot reaches forward and grabs the heel of a shoe ("clink"). Sometimes it's so bad that the horse gets a bleeding sore on the outside of its pastern or small cuts on the heel bulbs of its front feet.

Racehorses are prone to more serious injuries caused by interference than pleasure horses. Racetrack farriers are experts at "getting the front feet out of the way" because "grabbing a quarter" is a serious injury for a racehorse.

Pleasure horses usually have gait interference problems if their conformation is faulty. The opportunities for "brushing" or intereference get worse when they are extremely tired and when they are being ridden by inexperienced or extra-heavy riders (who are heavy on the bit or cause their horses to lose collection and go on the forehand).

Always examine your horse's feet carefully after riding. Keep minor cuts and sores medicated. If you are concerned about interference, talk to your farrier about possible solutions and consider sending your horse out for training with a professional.

HOOF WALL CRACKS

Your horse's feet might have small, superficial cracks in them that do not cause lameness. The type of cracks to worry about are called "stress fractures of the hoof wall." They are the result of a physical imbalance in the hoof, abnormal weight-bearing, or an inherent weakness in the toe or hoof wall caused by injury to the coronet.

Cracks in the hoof wall.

When your horse's hoof wall fractures, seek immediate medical and farrier care. This problem is out of your realm. Most of the treatment will come from the farrier, but if the crack is infected or causing lameness, medication might be necessary.

In some cases, minor surgery is done to clean out the crack and make sure that a new hoof wall can grow down in one continuous piece.

Wall cracks, particularly medial quarter cracks, can become a chronic problem. Usually, the horse needs to have the foot reoriented, and it can take a year or so to grow a proper new foot. Be patient with a horse recovering from a serious toe or wall crack. Even though the horse appears sound, it might not be ready for hard work.

HOOF WALL SEPARATIONS

Hoof wall disease can affect all breeds of horses, and all ages, although cases in young horses are very rare. Until a few years ago, this problem was rarely documented in the United States outside of a few very wet southern states, especially in Florida, where the problem was often deemed a "yeast infection."

In the study of hoof wall disease, no one really knows whether an organism from the air, the earth, or water invades the hoof wall or if conditions in the hoof wall become imbalanced and an ordinary organism becomes an opportunistic agent. Many problems can affect the integrity of the hoof-to-coffin bone bond. Think of the bond as having three parts: the bone, the linkage material (laminae), and the hoof wall. A problem in any of the three parts will make the foot unstable.

Tendon problems, particularly problems of the deep digital flexor tendon, affect the bone and can be at the root of a separation (see the previous section that describes flexural deformity). Laminitis is the most common way for the bond itself to be compromised (see Chapter 4 for more information about laminitis). Problems of the hoof wall also cause separations.

Benign hoof wall separation occurs naturally while others are created mechanically, by improper trimming, shoeing, or neglect. An overlong toe creates an exaggerated lever action in the foot whenever the coffin joint flexes. In such a case, the horn tubules are constantly being bent and thereby weakened or broken. Stress fractures (cracks) often result, but separation can result as well.

In the worst cases, hoof walls are "eaten alive" by "keratinolytic microorganisms," aggressive organisms of unknown origin, named by Professor Chris Pollitt, a research scientist at the University of Queensland in Australia. There seem to be no predictive parameters for knowing when or if a horse will be affected by the damaging keratinolytic microorganisms. Sometimes only one horse in a barn will be infected, and sometimes the resulting hoof wall separation occurs in only one foot of that horse. Curiously, the separation problems frequently affect show horses that receive the best of care.

Untreated, hoof wall disease can spread quickly inside the

foot and destroy enough of the inner hoof wall so that a condition develops that mimics mechanical laminitis. If you tap gently on the hoof wall with a farrier's driving hammer, you will hear that it sounds hollow underneath. The coffin bone might become unstable and even rotate. Serious lameness can result.

Hoof wall disease is sometimes called "white line disease." The disease is a condition that affects the inner hoof wall, which lies directly outside the white line, when you look at the bottom of the foot. Other names for the same disease include seedy toe (in the UK) and hollow wall disease. Horsemen in Australia sometimes use the term seedy toe if the case is a serious problem while they call more benign cases white line fever. More research on this disease should be done, to clinically recreate it in the laboratory, so it can be classified — and cured. In the meantime, this problem has stymied many a farrier and veterinarian. Over the course of just a few weeks, the time between shoeing appointments, a horse's hoof wall can be undermined so badly that the coffin bone rotates and permanent lameness results.

Owners with horses exhibiting signs of white line disease should press their farriers and veterinarians for the most current information on prevention and treatment available on this debilitating problem (see the entry on seedy toe).

Prevention: Avoid soaking the horse's feet. Avoid placing the horse in pastures or stabling that subject it to extremes of wet/dry conditions, especially if the horse has had problems with separations before. Always ask your farrier to let you know if any irregularities are present in the hoof wall or the white line. Keep your horse on a frequent shoeing schedule, even if the shoes are only to be reset. Keep the feet dry and clean. Many farriers will fill in old nail holes as a precaution, because they think the holes allow moisture to get inside the hoof wall. Evaluate your stall cleaning regimen to consider whether you need to lime the stall more frequently. Make sure that all wet spots in the stall are eliminated, right down to the flooring. Remove soiled bedding every day so that ammonia does not build up in the remaining bedding.

Warning signs: Farriers sometimes notice a widened white line or separation inside the white line, usually in the toe or quarters. The hoof wall might appear to be bulged or flared in the separated area. With any signs of hoof wall separation, watch for loose shoe clinches. The sole might seem to be migrating outward toward the edge of the hoof wall, often covering the defect. Through most of these changes, the horse usually will not be lame.

Hoof wall disease signs include a liquid exudate (discharge) that might look gray, white, or like black gunk; or diseased tissue sloughing off in the separation area. Liquid or solid, the "gunk" smells terrible. Remember that more than one foot can be infected. In early stages, there will be no sign of lameness. Caution: On radiographs, hoof wall problems often look identical to laminitis problems.

Treatment: Remember that the inner hoof wall can only grow down from the coronary band. The damaged wall can never "grow back" or reattach.

The body of knowledge about hoof wall separation cases is growing every day. Many cases of what is called "white line disease" are not that at all. Closer examination of such cases show mechanical separations or minor defects in the wall with a discharge. True hoof wall disease smells bad!

Many folk remedies are practiced on horses with white line disease including soaking the affected feet in the following secret potions: formaldehyde, iodine, bleach, gasoline, plant root killer, vinegar, volcanic ash, tea tree oil, (and many combinations of these caustic liquids). None of them has been proven to work. Some of these home remedies are much more dangerous to the horse than its hoof wall disease!

In field trials, applications of Merthiolate and 10% benzyl peroxide have been documented to be the most effective agents. Both can be applied topically to the horse's feet on a daily basis. When you hear tales of the success of some folk remedy, you have to wonder whether or not the separation was just a mechanical problem or a minor hoof wall defect rather than true hoof wall disease.

In the early stages of hoof wall disease and in relatively benign cases, trimming away the diseased tissue to clean out the affected area then packing it with cotton soaked in Merthiolate to prevent further spreading might be sufficient treatment to prevent further hoof-wall damage. A shoe is applied to hold the packing in place. In an aggressive case, there is no way of knowing for sure if all the affected tissue was removed. Left on its own inside a nice moist wall, the keratinolytic microorganism can spread quickly.

Most veterinarians and farriers agree that the only success-ful treatment for hoof wall disease is removal of all infected tissues, from the outside in. There are two ways to get in: from the ground up or from the outer wall in.

From the outer wall in means that a special pair of "half round" hoof nippers or a mechanical drill will be used burrow through parts of the hoof wall, down to the inner wall. Once the window has been made, the inner wall will be "debrided" of all diseased tissue. Following the debridement, a heart-bar shoe is usually applied to help stabilize the foot and provide support. If a great deal of hoof wall has been removed, nailing options are few. In such cases, a glue-on shoe makes an excellent alternative. Multiple clips also help keep the packing, pad, and shoe in place.

In cases of true hoof wall disease, the debrided hoof area should not be covered with hoof repair compound, since that will create a warm environment conducive to spreading the disease, if any infected tissue remains in the foot.

Merthiolate will stain the affected tissues and show any areas that need to be treated. Each stained area should be cut away and removed.

A hoof-growth supplement will provide a range of nutrients designed to speed growth of healthy new hoof wall. Popular brands include Farriers Formula, Grand Hoof, and Hoof Rite.

KERATOMA

"Keratoma" sounds vaguely like the name of a famous race-horse whose accomplishments you've forgotten. When you hear the word bantered around in a diagnosis of your horse's lameness, you should pay attention.

A keratoma is a mass of keratinous cells inside the hoof wall. The fibrous proteins that make the cells of the hard, horny part of the hoof are keratin. When such cells form as they should, the horse continues to grow healthy hooves. When such cells grow together inside the hoof wall, they form a mass much like a cancer tumor that is lodged between the horny outer wall and the white line. It is not malignant, but it can cause serious lameness, particularly since the lameness mimics an abscess or coffin bone frac-

The white lump on the inside of the hoof wall is a keratoma.

ture. If left inside the wall, it will continue to grow causing pressure and it will eventually displace the coffin bone.

Keratomas are not related to any other problem in the foot, including white line disease. They are self-contained and will not regrow after they are removed by surgery.

Most vets and farriers have favorite keratoma stories. It is an unusual lameness problem, and the size of the tumor inside the foot — and its location — makes its removal an unusual task.

Treatment: A keratoma will be visible on a radiograph. It must be removed to prevent damage inside the foot. The horse might need to be anesthetized. Simple incisions with an electric burr drill will be made in the wall on either side of the tumor. Wall stripping is the normal procedure (a narrow but tall section of hoof wall is lifted off the hoof capsule), but if the keratoma is close to the ground surface, it might be possible to transect the toe at the sole juncture and remove the mass. Most horses recover quickly after surgery.

If your horse has just had a keratoma removed, it will need special shoeing to support its foot until new hoof wall can grow down. The foot must be kept stable, particularly if the coronet is weakened by the loss of a long strip of wall.

NAVICULAR TYPE LAMENESS

Most lamenesses in the foot have a simple cause and effect: an injury or structural shortcoming creates a condition that eventually causes pain. If the source of the pain is not immediately obvious, your veterinarian can use nerve blocks, probes, and radiographs of the foot to determine what area is painful.

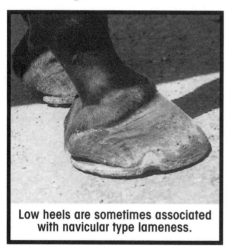

Low heels are sometimes associated with navicular type lameness.

One of the most common groups of lamenesses in the foot are those centered in the back of the foot, from the navicular bone area to the bulbs of the heels. Using hoof testers and diagnostic nerve blocks, the veterinarian can prove that the back part of the foot is the source of the pain. Sometimes a more precise diagnosis is not possible.

At the root of this group of conditions are characteristic foot structures, usually including a flat or dropped sole, heels that have collapsed and look "low" on the foot compared to the toe, swollen heel bulbs, or perhaps no outward abnormality at all.

Navicular type lameness is frustrating for the owner, who wants an answer to what is wrong with the horse and when (and if) the horse will be sound again. It is frustrating for the veterinarian, who might see distinct outward signs or radiographic signs, but not be able to say for certain what is causing the pain. It is frustrating for the farrier, who might have a limit in the range of trimming changes that can be done to a foot, or a limit to the shoe styles that can be applied to a certain shaped foot.

Navicular type lameness can be an acute problem that responds to treatment and then disappears completely, or it can be a permanent, low-grade unsoundness that will always require complex shoeing and trimming, medication, and physical therapy to keep the horse comfortable. Some horses never completely regain their previous athletic potential. Unfortunately, this is a crippling condition for some horses.

If your horse has or has had bouts of navicular type lameness, it is important to rule out what did NOT cause the problem. Radiographs are expensive, but they do disclose traumatic injuries to the foot like a fractured navicular bone. One of the most frustrating aspects of navicular lameness is that radiographs can show signs of arthritis or degenerative changes at the back of the coffin joint where the navicular bone sits, but those same irregularities are sometimes seen in the radiographs of sound horses.

Most navicular horses respond, at least temporarily, to changes in shoeing. However, structures within the foot, particularly the digital cushion, cartilages, and blood supply, might have been weakened and the horse has difficulty staying sound. A long layoff might be needed, but there is no guarantee that the foot can be restored to its former level of function.

Navicular type lameness is disastrous for a horse that is being sold, since it can discourage prospective buyers and wreak havoc at a pre-purchase exam. Veterinarians admit frustration to "making the call" on a horse's suitability for purchase, and many horses that fail exams end up excelling as athletes, while others, who seem only to have a temporary lameness, are left permanently unsound.

Navicular syndrome is the largest cause of lameness in performing horses, and the most difficult to manage. Prepare yourself for a long-term education in foot anatomy, shoeing, and physical therapy. Evaluate the horse's potential, your needs, and the horse's well-being. Assemble the best team of professionals you can to help you keep your horse sound.

Prevention: It is hard to think of a breed of horse that is not prone to this type of lameness. The condition is often made worse by infrequent shoeing and trimming, or neglect of hoofcare, but it may also show up in horses that have received top-level care all their lives.

Warning signs: Intermittent lameness, or low-grade lameness that slowly compromises the horse's willingness to perform or exert itself. Feet seem to suddenly "collapse" on the shoe, so that the heels are at a lower angle than the toe. Heels actually can curl under the horse, or to one side.

Treatment: Your veterinarian will evaluate the horse using flexion tests, nerve blocks, and radiographs. If nuclear scanning is available, that might be used, too. Pain medication can be used to get the horse through an initial bout of lameness,

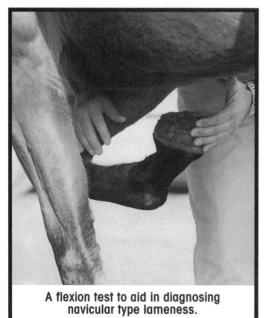

A flexion test to aid in diagnosing navicular type lameness.

or be prescribed for long-term use. Coffin joint injections are a common option, since the navicular bone sits at the back of the joint, and since research has shown that some of the coffin joint fluid will "spill" into the navicular area. Injecting a contrast medium into the bursa (sac) of the navicular bone and subsequent radiographs will disclose imperfections in the sac that indicate adhesions between the navicular bone and the deep digital flexor tendon that runs beneath it. Your veterinarian might be aware of new diagnostic media or treatment options that might help your horse.

Farriers are put under a great deal of pressure to reverse the signs of navicular lameness. They are asked to perform miracles by changing the way they trim or shoe the horse. It might take several shoeings to see any results from shoeing changes. The farrier might need to "tweak" the shoeing between regular visits. Egg bar shoes have always been the first thing farriers try. Pads are the second thing. Some horses benefit from simplifying the shoes, particularly when horses have been wearing drive-in studs or have trailers on their shoes. Instead of needing a miracle shoeing job, your horse might need a simpler shoe!

Many gimmicks are available to change heel angles temporarily or adjust weight bearing points on the horse's foot. Proceed with caution, and don't be a victim of false hope from a temporary aid. Always wait several weeks before extolling the virtues of a new shoeing trick, since many "cures" are soon left in the arena dust.

OSTEOMYELITIS

Osteomyelitis is one of the most debilitating lamenesses a horse can develop. Almost any bone can be affected, but in the foot, osteomyelitis generally is seen in the coffin bone. It means, literally, "infection leading to loss (or death) of bone tissue." It occurs most often as an after-effect of a severe puncture wound or damage to the coffin bone from severe laminitis. Once destroyed, bone tissue cannot be repaired. The damage to the bone is usually visible on a radiograph. Any diagnosis of this condition should come from a veterinarian and is cause for serious concern.

PEDAL OSTEITIS

Pedal osteitis literally means "inflammation of the pedal (coffin) bone." It is a hoof condition which, along with navicular syndrome, is a diagnostic dance in the dark. The symptoms are there. The radiographic evidence might be visible, but pinpointing the exact source of pain to the coffin bone is hard to do.

Technically, pedal osteitis is a chronic condition causing intermittent lameness. It might make the horse habitually tender in the feet. A simple way to think of how pedal osteitis affects a horse is to compare its sore feet to bald tires on a car. The wheels keep going around and as long as the tires have air, everything is fine, but if you take that car over a bumpy mountain road (or ride the horse over rough terrain), you are increasing the chances of a blowout, or in the horse's case, a flareup of lameness. Ride the car on smooth roads, and the tires may last longer.

Prevention: There is no real way to prevent pedal osteitis, as it is probably a condition secondary to other problems in the foot, such as flat feet, laminitis, chronic bruising, and abscesses.

Treat all lameness problems with diligence and speed. Don't wait to see if the problems will go away by themselves. If a horse needs a rest, give it plenty. If the horse is prone to hoof injuries, keep an eye on the surfaces on which it is worked. Make sure the farrier is aware of the horse's problems, particularly if you change farriers often. Watch for news of any new products that might help your footsore horse, and ask your farrier about them. He or she may roll his eyes and think you have been brainwashed by advertising claims, but you may hit on something that your farrier just learned about at a clinic or lecture and you could hear a hopeful, "Well, yeah, we could try that..."

If your horse shows repeated lameness and a footsore attitude, your veterinarian finally might recommend that you get radiographs that will show the perimeter of the coffin bone. That way, the vet can check for demineralization. Be aware that a sound horse's radiograph might show you even more irregularities in the coffin bone's solar margin than a lame horse's radiographs. The difference is that the sound horse is not bothered by the problem. Your horse might have a lower threshold of pain, or the angle of its hoof might be different enough to exert more pressure on the coffin bone. Also, the solar margin of a coffin bone naturally deteriorates with a horse's age and use.

Don't buy a horse that has radiographic evidence of pedal osteitis and a history of intermittent lameness. If you are told that the horse has been diagnosed with pedal osteitis but that it is being managed, proceed with caution. If your horse care budget is smaller than that of the current owner, it may mean a difference in the kind of environment, nutrition, stabling, and farrier care given to the horse.

Warning signs: The signs of pedal osteitis are no different from any other solar lameness, such as subsolar abscess, or bruising.

Treatment: Your veterinarian will use nerve blocks to isolate the source of pain and rule out other causes of lameness. You might be asked to write up a lameness history. It should include dates that injuries and periods of lameness occurred, plus all of your records about bruises, abscesses, and white line disease. It may be helpful to compare the placement and condition of the coffin bone shown in old radiographs against a newer set of radiographs. You will need to develop a long-term hoofcare management plan for the horse, and you must be realistic about the horse's future as an athlete. This will be a high-maintenance horse to keep shod and comfortable. Shoeing adjustments may make the horse more comfortable. Pain medication will be helpful, too.

In extreme cases, neurectomy may be recommended. You will need to discuss your options with your veterinarian.

QUITTOR

Abscesses that drain at the coronary band are a common problem in horses. Quittor is not.

Quittor is a precise name for a precise infection in the lateral cartilage, usually just on one side of the foot. A puncture wound or laceration, or even repeated coronet wounds from gait interference, can allow an infection to take root in the cartilage area. Then pus from the infected area seeks a way out of the foot, and breaks out at the coronet. It looks exactly like an abscess. However, an abscess heals quickly and goes away. Quittor is likely to appear to heal, then breaks loose again.

Fortunately, quittor is a relatively rare problem in horses, but it is an extremely serious one. A veterinarian will have to open the coronet and remove infected tissue from the cartilage. A long recovery, while the coronet heals, is to be expected, and the horse's long-term soundness may be compromised. Always make sure that any penetrating wound to the foot is properly treated by a veterinarian and fully healed before the horse returns to training.

SEEDY TOE

In Britain, the term "seedy toe" means hoof wall disease. In America, it means a stretched or irregular white line. If someone brings up the subject of seedy toe, make sure that you are both talking about the same condition! In America, what we call seedy toe is usually an after-effect of laminitis. The stretched white line is the separated area of the hoof wall growing down. As the new hoof wall grows down from above, the white line should improve with each successive hoof trimming.

Seedy toe is a condition of the foot, but is usually not a direct cause of lameness. It can make it difficult to nail a shoe onto a foot, but the white line behind the quarters is rarely affected.

Seedy toe often looks worse than it really is. As long as the foot is properly trimmed, the problem will grow out. The area should be kept protected so that dirt and infection do not find their way into the hoof wall to cause abscesses, and so that moisture will not create a welcome environment for true hoof wall disease.

SELENIUM POISONING

Chronic selenium toxicity brings on a rare, but severe, hoof problem. Selenium is a trace mineral found naturally in most parts of the United States. Horses have a dietary requirement for a certain amount of this mineral, but an excess acts like poison, causing a toxic reaction. Many brands of feed and supplements include enough selenium to meet a horse's daily requirements. This is one very important reason why you should not double up or combine feed supplements!

Outward signs of selenium toxicity are a dull coat and a horizontal separation of the hoof wall. In severe cases, the hoof capsules might slough (fall off). In such cases, selenium toxicity is sometimes mistaken with other diseases that result in laminitis. In some cases, the foot looks like it has two hoof walls, a new inner one and the old outer one. Subsolar abscesses and chronic lameness are frequent side effects.

Prevention: Read the contents labels on your horse's feed and supplements. Add the amounts of selenium up then ask your vet if that amount meets, but does not exceed, the horse's needs.

SUPERFICIAL FLEXOR TENDON INJURY (BOWED TENDON)

There is no documentation that any sort of corrective shoeing can speed recovery from bowed or ruptured tendons, even when the horse is suffering from a low bow and the shape of the foot seems to have contributed to the injury.

Treatment: Most veterinarians will suggest that any sort of special performance-related shoes be removed (i.e., toe grabs, raised heels, sliding plates). Then the foot should be trimmed to create as natural as possible hoof/pastern alignment. Horses with foot problems should be shod with the flattest, least manipulative shoe. Raised heel shoes, cutting down the heels, and trying to increase or decrease toe angles out of the normal range are not helpful in most cases.

SUPPORT LIMB LAMENESS OR BREAKDOWN

When a horse has been in an accident or is recovering from surgery, it is natural for you to focus your attention on the injured leg. After all, you are spending hours medicating and bandaging the leg, constantly monitoring its swelling or the progress in wound healing. It is easy to ignore the opposite leg. Don't. That leg will be bearing more of the horse's weight. You may not notice when it changes in appearance. After all, you cannot use the injured leg as a basis for comparison, since the "healthy" leg might not look swollen compared to a leg wrapped in multiple layers of cotton! Also, lameness in the support leg might not be discernible, since the horse is obviously lame in the beginning from the injury!

Despite widespread education on the care of overloaded support (non-injured) legs, horses continually suffer. Leg fractures, bowed tendons, and ligament injuries are common problems that predispose a horse to support limb lameness.

Prevention: Veterinarians include the care of an opposing support limb right along with their treatment plan for the injured leg. Their goal is to prevent support limb lameness and breakdown. They routinely will "prescribe" that the farrier provide the support limb with a full support shoe or some type of frog support. Your vet might suggest that the injured horse be outfitted with a suspensory support boot ("sports medicine boot") during stall rest. Many veterinary hospital clinics put injured horses in belly slings to avoid overloading uninjured legs. Just because the horse is laid up, do not scrimp on hoof monitoring and cleaning, and simple massage or stretching. Learn how to do basic suppling, massage, and stretching exercises. Consider using a "turbolator" boot occasionally on the good leg.

Warning signs: Classic signs of lameness range from heat in the leg or hoof wall to a bounding or rapid digital pulse, swelling, constant shifting of weight, movement of hind limbs forward under the body (if a front limb is injured), changes in foot shape, stretching of the white line, and collapsing of the sole. Noticeable changes in the growth of the hoof (i.e., less growth in toe, more growth in heel) might result as well.

Treatment: Farriers might apply a built-up shoe on the support limb to make it equal height if the injured limb is in a brace or cast that makes it longer. Support limb shoeing may be done at the time of treatment of the major injury, to spare the horse increased pain; a common example is fracture surgery, where a support shoe is applied to the uninjured leg while the horse is under anesthesia. When resetting support shoes, it may be necessary to sedate the horse, since weight often cannot be borne on the opposite injured leg. Slings are also sometimes used during shoeing.

THRUSH

Ask a group of horse owners what the most common foot problem is, and most would surely answer "Thrush!" in unison...and wrinkle their noses at the same time. As you say the word "thrush," you can almost smell it! Thrush is often called "athlete's foot in horses." It is a bacterial infection caused by poor management. An important part of the care regime to cure a horse of thrush is to examine its environment in order to eliminate excess moisture. It is found in horses kept in muddy pens or dirty stalls. Paradoxically, thrush also shows up in the best show barns. There, its prevalence can be linked to the predominantly wet environment of barns, paddocks, and show barn aisles (which have become the show horses' equivalent of dirty locker rooms).

A horse can have thrush in one or all of its feet. The problem is not contagious from one horse to another and is not spread to humans.

Warning signs: Perhaps one of these days, you will be cleaning out your horse's feet and the point of the hoof pick in the sulcus of the frog will draw blood. Or the horse will start to flinch when you are cleaning around the frog. Or, worse yet, you pick up the horse's foot and are horrified to smell what you are sure is rotten flesh. Could gangrene have set in? The frog is flaking and there is a runny black serum around the frog, usually right in the cleft and around the tip or in the back, at the base of the triangle.

Treatment: Many commercial medications are available to treat thrush. A daily topical application to the sole and frog will clear up the problem in short order.

Before you begin to medicate the frog, think about how your horse's feet are shod and trimmed. Some farriers, particularly those who work at a racetrack, pare down the frog routinely, using a curved blade hoof knife. Track farriers claim that this prevents thrush. It might, but it also can weaken the foot.

The so-called "natural foot" would have a full frog with deep pockets around all the edges of the frog. Those pockets need to be cleaned daily because they are natural gardens in which thrush can grow. If your horse has a full frog and smells of thrush, call you farrier and see if you can schedule a frog-trim. This can be done without disturbing the shoe. Your farrier will use the hooked end of curved-blade and just trim away overhanging bits of frog, making it easier for you to clean around the foot.

Thrush's favorite target is a foot with contracted heels and a shriveled up frog. Thrush can live happily ever after inside the nooks and crannies of that kind of frog.

In recent years, farriers have reported an increase in what they call "deep sulcus thrush." This is a chronic thrush that seems to be resistant to the over-the-counter medications. Sometimes the deep sulcus thrush infection spreads into deeper tissues making it nearly impossible to cure simply by applying medication. Cutting away the diseased tissue then packing the foot requires the combined efforts of a veterinarian and farrier.

Even though thrush is common and quite curable, it can become a chronic problem in some horses. An especially bad place for thrush to grow is in the fissure between the separated heels of a sheared-heel foot. Thrush can get out of control and "eat" its way into the sensitive frog or under the sole. Once this happens, the horse will go lame. You will need to keep medicating the foot on a regular schedule.

Three-Dimensional Appreciation of the Horse's Foot

New ideas in the study of the horse's foot don't come along every day. The study of horses' feet had its heyday around the turn of the century. It wasn't until the 1980s that a revival of interest in the foot encouraged biomechanics and pathology professionals to apply new technologies to the ancient art of hoofcare. Advances in human biomechanics were transferable to the horse, and the monetary value of horses was reaching new peaks, so researchers found an eager audience.

No audience was more eager for the information than the "new breed" of farriers, young professionals bent on combining traditional skills with contemporary science. To the scientific knowledge laid down by research at major universities in America, Europe, Japan, and Australia, farriers began publishing their own observations, experiences, and theorems.

The best and the brightest of these early "hoof renaissance" theorems came from Great Britain. A farrier educator in formal training programs in England and Ireland, and a champion competition farrier, David Duckett FWCF pulled together the foot into a tidy package and opened it up for the world to see.

Duckett's idea was that the foot, out there at the end of the horse's leg, had many more unique properties than many people were willing to recognize. First, the foot could regenerate its structures if they were injured or even lopped off in an accident. A horse could grow a new frog…but it couldn't grow a new tongue or new ears. Somehow, the new frog ended up being in the right place on the foot and of the right shape so that it could function properly. Duckett suggested that a larger "order of things" was at work in the hoof than the old masters had touched upon in their turn-of-the-century tomes.

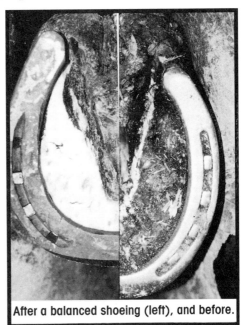

After a balanced shoeing (left), and before.

A foot had length and width as qualities by which to judge its shape, but it also had the third dimension, depth. Duckett started people thinking about the shape of the coffin bone inside the hoof capsule, about the flexion of the coffin joint, about the interconnectedness of the interior structures, and about the uncanny vertical alignment of certain structures in the foot.

Duckett's seminars gained notoriety with a simple experiment. He lectured on a position on the frog that he (at first jokingly) called "Duckett's Dot." The name stuck! The point was (and still is) about three-eighths of an inch behind the tip of the trimmed frog on a normal-sized foot. Using a leg taken from a cadaver, Duckett would drill a hole right through the hoof capsule at the dot, until the tip of the drill bit emerged in the coronet area.

He then dissected the foot by simply splitting it down the

centerline created by the tip of the frog.

The drill hole went through the frog, into the attachment of the deep digital flexor tendon at the base of the coffin bone. The drill hole bisected the coffin bone, emerging at the extensor process, continuing up through the coffin joint and attachment of the common digital extensor tendon, through the blood supply of the hoof wall in the coronary band, and out through the coronet. Was it a freak of nature that all these important structures line up on a vertical axis...or is the foot truly a wonder of the horse's evolution, as so many paleontologists have always suggested?

Coincidentally, the "dot" described by Duckett was also the exact point where the tip of a heart bar shoe sits on the frog.

No matter how much the perimeter of a foot changes in shape — distortion from flares, long toes, underrun heels, club feet, whatever the problem — the center point can always be found, and a balanced foot created around it. By finding "the dot," farriers began using an exterior reference point on the foot to help them understand where the interior structures were located. Guesswork was eliminated. The foot seemed much more logical.

Since 1986, when Duckett began teaching people about the dot, hoof studies have exploded. The foot is approachable, understandable, and more manageable. Volumes have been written, using Duckett's work as a launching pad. Volumes more need to be written. But we have created a simple language to understand the foot, which you should be able to assimilate into your own practical management of your horse's feet.

If you can remember only one thing, remember this: the foot down there at the end of the leg is like a pendulum. The pendulum swings smoothly if it is a uniform shape, evenly balanced left to right and front to back. But, in addition, the stem of the pendulum has to be inserted in just the right point for a perpetual swing.

So it is with the horse's foot. Look at it from side to side.

Look at it from front to back. But also look at it from above, knowing that the leg needs a sturdy foot in just the right place to make strides as effortless as possible and avoid unnecessary jarring and injury.

INDEX

ACKNOWLEDGMENTS

Information and advice provided in this text were collected from the ongoing work of the consulting editors of *Hoofcare & Lameness: The Journal of Equine Foot Science.*

FARRIERS

Alan Bailey, Doug Butler, Emil Carre, Simon Curtis, Bruce Daniels, David Duckett, Bernard Duvernay, David Farley, Paul Goodness, Alison Hayes, Alice Johnson, Edward Martin, Grant Moon, Rob Sigafoos, Allen Smith, Michael Wildenstein.

VETERINARIANS

Osamu Aoki, Olin Balch, Robert Bowker, Hilary Clayton, Jean-Marie Denoix, Sue Dyson, William Moyer, Chris Pollitt, Tracy Turner, Janice Young.

Special thanks to Beth Garner.

Hoofcare & Lameness is a subscription-based interdisciplinary professional journal with advanced information on hoofcare topics. For more information, write to H&L, PO Box 6600, Gloucester, MA 01930 USA.

RECOMMENDED READINGS

Clayton, H. Conditioning Sport Horses. Saskatoon: Sport Horse Publications, 1991.

Hertsch, B, Hoppner, S and Dallmer, H. The Hoof. Salzhausen-Putensen Helmuth Dallmer, 1996.

Hill, C and Klimesh, R. Maximum Hoof Power. New York: Howell Book House, 1994.

Hood, DM, Wagner, IP and Jocobson, AC. Proceedings of the Hoof Project 1997. College Station, Texas: Texas A&M University, 1997.

King, C and Mansmann, R. Equine Lameness. Grand Prairie Equine Research Inc., 1997.

Leach, D, Moyer, W, and Pollitt, CC. Equine Lameness and Foot Conditions, Refresher Course for Veterinarians. Post Graduate Committee in Veterinary Science, University of Sydney, 1990.

Mansmann, RA and Miller, PS. Instructions for Equine Clients. St. Louis: Mosby-Year Book, Inc., 1995.

Pollitt, CC. Color Atlas of the Horse's Hoof. London: Mosby-Wolfe, 1995.

Pollitt, CC, Young, JM, Pascoe, R, and Swan, K. Equine Foot Science. St Lucia, Veterinary Science Postgraduate Committee of the School of Veterinary Science, University of Queensland, 1992.

Ramey, DW. Concise Guide To Navicular Syndrome in the Horse. New York: Howell Book House, 1997.

Rooney, JR. The Lame Horse rev, updated, and expanded. Neenah: Russell Meerdink Co., 1996.

Stashak, TS. Adams' Lameness in Horses, 4th ed. Philadelphia: Lea & Febiger, 1987.

Stashak, TS and Hill, C. Horseowner's Guide To Lameness. Baltimore: Williams & Wilkins, 1995.

Yovich, JV. Ed. The Veterinary Clinics of North America: Equine Practice: The Equine Foot. Philadelphia, April 1989.

Equine Foot sites on the Internet

The Horse Interactive: http://www.thehorse.com

Hoofcare & Lameness: http://www.hoofcare.com

The Holistic Horse: http://www. holistichorse.com

The Haynet: http://www.haynet.net

American Farrier's Association: http://www.amfarriers.com

American Association of Equine Practitioners
 Client Education articles:
 http://www.aaep.org/client.htm

The Equine Connection: The National AAEP Locator
 Service:
 http://www.getadvm.com/equcon.html

Sport Horse Biomechanics and Effects of Shoeing studies
 at Michigan State University:
 http://www.cvm.msu.edu/dressage

The Hoof Project at Texas A&M:
 http://www.cvm.tamu.edu/hoof

Picture Credits

CHAPTER 1
Hoofcare & Lameness, 13; Anne M. Eberhardt, 22, 24.

CHAPTER 2
Anne M. Eberhardt, 30, 38.

CHAPTER 3
Anne M. Eberhardt, 43-45, 49, 52, 55;
John Blombach/*Hoofcare & Lameness, 47, 58.*

CHAPTER 4
Anne M. Eberhardt, 62-64, 82; Alan Bailey, 69; Janet Douglas, 69; Chris Pollitt, 69; John Blombach, 70; Emil Carre, 71; Bernard Duvernay, 71; Alice Johnson, 72; Bruce Chase, 72; Burney Chapman, 72, 85; color photos courtesy of *Hoofcare & Lameness*; Kendra Bond, 81.

CHAPTER 5
Hoofcare & Lameness, 107, 114, 121, 122; Joe Painter, 113;
Anne M. Eberhardt, 116, 124.

ADDENDUM
Chris Pollitt and John Arkley/*Hoofcare & Lameness,* 135.

COVER/BOOK DESIGN — SUZANNE C. DEPP
ILLUSTRATIONS — ROBIN PETERSON
COVER PHOTOGRAPH — CROWELL HADDEN, JR.

About the Author

Fran Jurga is the publisher of *Hoofcare & Lameness, The Journal of Equine Therapy*, a quarterly publication devoted to the dissemination of technical information about the care of horses' feet and legs and the treatment of lamenesses of all kinds.

Jurga first became aware of the demand for information  about horses' lameness problems while she was working as a publicist for the Tufts University College of Veterinary Medicine. She has worked as the editor of the *American Farriers Journal* and writes a monthly column, "Step by Step," for *The Horse: Your Guide to Equine Health*, in addition to compiling information for the popular Web site, http://www.hoofcare.com.

Fran Jurga

Jurga's pursuit of information for her readers has taken her to work with horses in Europe, New Zealand, and Australia, as well as North America. She conducts informal "hoof awareness" seminars and arranges speaking engagements for veterinarians and farriers for lecture organizers.

"I found that my role as a hoofcare information specialist has enabled me to give something back to horses for all they have done for me in my life," Jurga says.

"I know that many of the people who buy *Understanding The Equine Foot* want to help horses whose athletic potential has been compromised by prior injury or lack of good footcare by previous owners," she adds. "I want to help these people help their horses. If I can, in some small way, I'll feel like I have done my job."

Jurga lives in Gloucester, Massachusetts.